The PRACTICE *of* WISDOM

The PRACTICE *of* WISDOM

An Inspired One Year Journey Through the Book of Proverbs

DIANE ZIERAU

XULON PRESS

Xulon Press
2301 Lucien Way #415
Maitland, FL 32751
407.339.4217
www.xulonpress.com

Paperback ISBN-13: 978-1-6628-0421-2
Ebook ISBN-13: 978-1-6628-0422-9

Dedication

To my Glorious and Generous Father,
my Defender,
my Peace,
my Rock and my Fortress,
Redeemer,
and the Lover of My Soul,
from Whom all good things have always and shall always come.

"When I discovered your words, I devoured them.
They are my joy and my heart's delight, for I bear your name,
O Lord God of Heaven's Armies."
~ Jeremiah 15:16 (NLT)

Table of Contents

Preface

"Don't turn your back on wisdom, for she will protect you. Love her, and she will guard you."
~Proverbs 4:6 (NLT)

*W*isdom is grace, love, truth, understanding and knowledge in action. It's the perfect balance that allows us to respond just right in any circumstance, leaving us feeling empowered, blessed, and with no reason to doubt ourselves. Expressing wisdom also blesses those around us to feel secure and confident as they witness well-spoken and timely responses that are born of truth.

Wisdom was with God from the very beginning, yet how many of us intentionally study wisdom for the purpose of growing ourselves into a person more aligned with God's will for us? Whether you are new to Scripture reading or have been doing it for years, this book is designed to help you do just that, by establishing a *practice* in wisdom.

We have often practiced a thing to position ourselves well for that next step. We practice perfecting an artistic skill that we love, to prepare for a new sports challenge, perhaps a chess tournament or spelling bee, or practice with a musical instrument that we'd love to master. In many cases the practice is for a set time with a specific goal in mind.

Let's look at the word *practice* as a noun, though, for the purpose of working in wisdom: as "a practice" to daily apply wisdom's concepts in our lives. Committing to *a practice* is a form of continually training ourselves, for a practice is an ongoing exercise that advances us in knowledge and, ideally, in the skill of a thing. It's clear in Hebrews 5:14 that we are able to train our minds through practice, *"But solid food is for full-grown men, for those whose senses and mental faculties are trained by practice to discriminate and distinguish between what is morally good and noble and what is evil and contrary either to divine or human law,"(AMPC).*

What better thing to advance our senses and mental faculties in than knowledge of the wisdom designed by God?

Wisdom is personified in the Book of Proverbs. She is referred to in the feminine and is often capitalized as a proper name throughout the book. Just as if she were our best friend, we see Wisdom's name as she calls out in the street, proactively seeking to draw in those that might otherwise pass her by. We read that she seeks those who desire insight, knowledge and understanding. She seeks to bring order to our very core, to impart confident knowing which results in wise action.

King Solomon was known as the wisest man of his time, and he penned most of the passages in Proverbs. 1 Kings 3:1-14 tells us how the Lord appeared to Solomon in a dream, asking him what he wanted God to give to him. Sit in the awesomeness of that opportunity for a moment: the Creator of the Universe initiated the conversation, asking the young man what he wanted! Solomon did not ask for material things or power but instead considered his own lack of experience and weakness to govern the great nation of Israel that God had set him over. He asked for what he believed he truly needed to accomplish his mission – an understanding heart with which to distinguish good and bad as he judged the people.

We read that the Lord was so pleased with Solomon asking for this wisdom that He gave him good beyond what he asked for: He blessed him with riches and honor that he did not seek out, and wisdom and understanding that would exceed all those that had gone before him and that would arise after him. What a beautiful expression of the Father's heart towards us! Know today that our Heavenly Father is good, His thoughts of us are for good, and He has plans for good towards us, to give us a future and a hope. He tells us so in Jeremiah 29:11.

The Wise Learn By Instruction

God highly valued Solomon's choice to seek wisdom and He highly values when we choose to seek it, too. The Scriptures tell us wisdom is to be valued above silver and gold. A key theme that Solomon repeats through many chapters is the wise person learns by instruction while the fool learns through consequence (Proverbs 1:29-32, 19:19, 21:11). Yes, we all have those times in our lives when we have placed ourselves in circumstances that teach us through consequence. Solomon speaks, though, of the fool who learns by no other means. She is not interested in investing the time to learn and grow by studying the words of knowledge in Scripture or he doesn't care to be instructed by true knowledge and understanding. Consider today with which of these learners you are more closely aligned: the fool or the wise? It can make all the difference for success in your life.

Have you been one who has learned only by consequence? I encourage you to change your story now. You can stop the pattern you've created for yourself and choose wisdom. Write yourself into a new story and choose to learn by instruction. James, the half-brother of Jesus, tells us that God shall give wisdom to anyone who asks for it in faith, believing that he shall receive it (James 1:5-6).

A Month, a Year, a Lifetime to Grow

The thirty-one chapters of the Book of Proverbs make it perfect for a one-month study, as if it's designed to encourage us to grow in wisdom, insight and understanding by meditating on one chapter each day. But what if we took that principle and made it more than just a one-month study? What if we made it a one-year, two-year, or lifetime *practice* to seek out the wisdom so beautifully depicted in the words and lessons of Proverbs?

What if you could write down, in one central place, your thoughts on the verses that speak to you each month as you read through the chapters?

What if you could measure your personal development in wisdom, knowledge, and understanding by having not only the words from Scripture but your progress for an entire year right at your fingertips?

What if you could build your own reference list by topic of the words of wisdom that speak to you and have it at the ready when needed for guidance, comfort, times of prayer, and meditation before God?

That long-lasting growth that is available to all, that great and eternal perspective infused into each of us through the study of wisdom, is my passion behind the writing of this book.

The Practice of Wisdom was born from my seeking a standalone book to share with others on the immeasurable benefits of incorporating wisdom from the Book of Proverbs into our lives. I have studied through Proverbs more times than I can count, and, as with all of Scripture, God is always so faithful to show me new and advancing concepts each time I read through it.

"Old" verses that I've read before speak to me in new ways, often to accompany the seasons of life – parenthood, grandparenthood, times of loss, comfort and gain – that I am advancing through.

"New" verses that I'd never taken notice of before pop out at me like bright neon signs directing me towards safety on a dark night.

Notes and dates are penned in the margins and across the pages of Proverbs in my Bible, memorializing the lessons of those verses and the quiet teaching of the Holy Spirit as He has spoken to my heart.

I'd love for all this and more to be your experience, too, and I've written this book so that you don't have to squeeze all those notes in tiny print into the margin of your Bible, or leave them written in a notebook where you may have to shuffle through page after page at some future date to find that special message spoken to you by God. This one-year journal study has been written that you may have a twelve-month continuous record of your progress in wisdom, all in one book that includes the Proverbs to read from, with room to record the thoughts God speaks to you and the direction He's giving you immediately following each chapter. The journal pages are designed for you to begin at any time, on any day, in any month of the year, and to cycle through an entire year from that point forward. You will have a one-year journey documented when you're complete – establishing your own insightful roadmap to wisdom, with the waypoints of each day noted.

Does studying the Book of Proverbs every day sound like a commitment with discipline you're not sure you have? Let me encourage you to take just one day at a time. Be intentional, desire this personal growth for yourself, believe you can do it. Ask God to show you the time and space where you can accomplish it, for He surely will answer you. This is so much richer than merely reading a chapter each day, it is a practice of sitting in the presence of God – of seeking His wisdom, His teaching, of hearing the voice of the Holy Spirit speak to your heart, and growing in your relationship with Him. What better goal could we ever have than developing a more intimate relationship with our Creator?

What if a day goes by and it doesn't happen? It's okay. Give yourself grace and pick up the next day with that day's reading. Don't look back, don't try to catch up, don't criticize yourself for what you didn't do. Just do what you are able to each day and advance forward. Matthew tells us in chapter 6, verse 34 of his gospel that each day's concerns are enough for that day. Let it be so. Blank spaces in your journal are okay.

Ask God for wisdom each day that you read. Trust that He is growing your knowledge of wisdom. Be aware of the opportunities to apply the understanding you gain and the principles of wisdom to life daily.

You'll find that you grow in confidence in your decision-making.

You'll find that you grow in situational insight.

You'll find the stressors that fly at you at those times when you might typically doubt yourself are silenced by the principles of God's wisdom because His wisdom has strengthened your very core.

You'll even see the people in your life in a new light and understand better how to draw boundaries for yourself and others.

You shall gain so much more than just these things, because God is the God of infinite possibilities and glorious destinies. What He plans for you is so unique and special that He wants you to walk freely in the fullness of it. Undoubtedly, wisdom is a steppingstone to freedom.

Be blessed, dear ones, as you begin your journey. Come along each day, exploring all that Wisdom has to offer and embrace her.

May you look back a year from now and see each treasured step as a precious gift from God on your advancing road through life.

~ Diane Zierau, 2020

Introduction

Enriching Your Life with this Book

This one-year journal is designed to be an active part of your life. To get the most from your experience, I encourage you to sit and read one chapter each day.

Chapters

*Y*ou'll see that the chapters of this book dedicated to daily reading of the Proverbs are named The First through The Thirty-First. Each chapter contains some thoughts to consider as well as the corresponding chapter from the Book of Proverbs. The thoughts are just a launchpad to usher you into a quiet, thoughtful time, or to find a starting place if journaling is new to you. The words I've written are not meant to supersede what God speaks to your heart, and I encourage you to always listen for what He is saying to you each day through Scripture.

To systematically read through Proverbs, read Chapter 1 on the first of each month, Chapter 2 on the second of each month, etc., and in this way you will continually read through the Book of Proverbs. You don't have to wait until the first of a month to begin studying; if you receive this book mid-month and are ready to start on the fifteenth, then start with Chapter 15 and continue with one chapter per day through the end of the month. You'll then turn to Chapter 1 (for the first of the month) as the next month begins.

Note that the daily chapters of Proverbs are taken from several versions of the Bible. These are the abbreviations used for the different Bible translations if reading the Bible is new to you:

- AMPC: Amplified Classic Bible
- ESV: English Standard Version
- NASB: New American Standard Bible
- NIV: New International Version
- NKJV: New King James Version
- NLT: New Living Translation

Journaling

At the end of each chapter are journal pages – one for each month of the year, for every chapter. I encourage you to write in them each day as you read through the book, noting what really speaks to you from Proverbs that day. Is there a lesson on wisdom or insight that particularly speaks to your heart? Perhaps a message on drawing boundaries with others? There certainly is a lot about contention, strife and healthy relationships between people in there. Maybe words of love and encouragement are speaking to you? Trust that whatever verse you feel impressed on your heart is coming from the Holy Spirit, write the verse and those accompanying thoughts down on the journal page for that day, pray what needs to be prayed and record that prayer, too, if you like.

I've been sitting with God and journaling for years now. I tend to spend that time with Him in the morning before daily activities begin – I think of it as my "compass time" when I receive direction for the day. Those have become some of the most precious hours of my life, sitting in His presence with His word before me, pen in hand, receiving truth and insight into my own life as I read through the Scriptures. I encourage you to find your right time and place each day to pursue a relationship with Him where you will grow, soak up His wisdom, and learn to confidently apply it in your life.

Your completed journal will reflect a year of entries from whenever you began, with your entries organized for you by chapter. Why does that matter? Back in the days of the Old Testament, the people of God were often instructed to construct an altar of rocks as remembrance to God's wonderful work at a place. Your journal stands as a sort of personal altar of remembrance to God's wonderful work in your life. It's important to have markers that document our growth and maturity, to see for ourselves that we've put in the effort to grow in our relationship with God, in our faith, and in character-building disciplines like understanding and wisdom. This gives us each a personalized, unique volume containing a year's worth of insights and lessons from God that often follows along with the events of our lives, as we set aside time to seek and receive His input daily. How beautiful that we can have this volume to look back through: we'll have a lasting record of how we've grown!

A Growing Relationship with God

Remember, God initiated the conversation with Solomon that led to his request for wisdom. What might God want to speak to us? Are we allowing that time each day to hear from Him? In 1 Chronicles 28:9, David tells Solomon, *"For the LORD sees every heart and knows every plan and thought. If you seek him, you will find him," (NLT)*. Seek Him through prayer as you turn to a new chapter of Proverbs each day. He will not turn you away.

I have five simple steps that I open with each morning as I read the words of Scripture.

1. I lay my hands over the pages of my bible and thank God for His word, which is awesome and endures forever (Isaiah 40:8). I allow myself to feel the gratitude and amazement over the words I will read – words written thousands of years ago, which have endured through countless generations to still be alive and in my hands today.
2. I pray that God would meet with me today.
3. I pray that He would speak to me through His word.
4. I pray He would teach me by His word.
5. I pray He would strengthen me by His word.

I believe, after praying these things, that He is faithful to answer.

Meditate on the Reading

Meditation is not a mysterious concept. King David, the author of so many of the Psalms, speaks of meditating several times. The ancient Hebrew word that we see translated as the word "meditate" in today's Bibles actually means to murmur to yourself. It is good that we ponder over and consider the words of Proverbs within ourselves. I encourage you to do your best to focus on what's being said in the words actually written on the page each day. Let preconceived notions, last week's sermon, what others have told you this should mean, all fall away and hear what the Holy Spirit – the Spirit of Truth (John 15:26, John 16:13, 1 John 5:6) – is saying to you.

Build a Topical Reference

Finally, there is a "Topical" area at the back of the book where you can build your own collection of verses from Proverbs that speak to you on certain subjects. Let's take love, for example. Write the word "Love" as the subject on one of these pages and then include any verses that speak to you about love just after it. You might want to do the same for other topics like forgiveness, insight, truth, the sluggard (oh yes, Proverbs has a lot to say about the sluggard!), or any other topic that you really want to focus on.

Embrace Wisdom as Your Companion!

Any moments spent studying wisdom are treasured moments that spark growth in us. God does not call us to just exist. He has called us to joy, He has called us to be an advancing people who express the gifts He has given us to the world around us, that they may know the fantastic journey of a life in Christ.

He has called us each to walk in a unique destiny. Wisdom is a most worthy companion to have by your side.

Blessings to you as you begin this journey through the Book of Proverbs!

The First

Purpose

"Let the wise listen to these proverbs and become even wiser. Let those with under-standing receive guidance by exploring the meaning in these proverbs and parables, the words of the wise and their riddles."
~Proverbs 1:5-6 (NLT)

The Book of Proverbs is considered part of the "wisdom literature" of Scripture. Wisdom literature goes beyond straight historical account, law and ritual to provide instruction into the human story of how we can best live life. Proverbs are, "...truths obscurely expressed, maxims, and parables," (Proverbs 1:1, AMPC) meaning the Proverbs are brief statements designed to be considered and explored, statements that convey universal truths for righteous living.

We start off with the necessary introductions and learn these are the proverbs of Solomon, David's son, and that Solomon is the King of Israel. Clearly, we know Solomon is the author of this portion of Proverbs, but the fact that he refers to his father, David, sets the stage for understanding.

King David was referred to by God as a man after his own heart in 1 Samuel 13:14. This is the same King David who, as a teenager, was the victor in the story of David versus Goliath. While David was a man who openly made mistakes, his heart toward God was clearly something noteworthy. That heart must have been evident in Solomon's upbringing.

Think of that power of influence as you read the words Solomon pens, understanding the impact our words, our actions, our way of living have, not only on those around us, but on generations to come.

Use the journal page for this month that follows the reading to write down any verses that speak to your heart and elaborate on them in your own words. What you write is just between you and God. Don't worry if you haven't had experience journaling or if you feel uncomfortable about your ability to write. Just put pen to the paper and write something. Draw a picture, if that's what speaks to you. Do it again tomorrow and then the next day. Persevere in your reading of these wise words and in listening for God's voice in them. That's how we begin to meditate on the characteristics of wisdom.

If you need a little help getting started, look closely at verses 2-5 and see what the purpose of this collection of writings is. You'll see that the Proverbs are written with intention, to help our development as mature human beings in relationship with God.

Blessings to you, friends, as we grow in truth together.

Proverbs Chapter 1
(NLT)

¹These are the proverbs of Solomon, David's son, king of Israel.

²Their purpose is to teach people wisdom and discipline, to help them understand the insights of the wise.

³Their purpose is to teach people to live disciplined and successful lives, to help them do what is right, just, and fair.

⁴These proverbs will give insight to the simple, knowledge and discernment to the young.

⁵Let the wise listen to these proverbs and become even wiser. Let those with understanding receive guidance ⁶by exploring the meaning in these proverbs and parables, the words of the wise and their riddles.

⁷Fear of the Lord is the foundation of true knowledge, but fools despise wisdom and discipline.

⁸My child, listen when your father corrects you. Don't neglect your mother's instruction.

⁹What you learn from them will crown you with grace and be a chain of honor around your neck.

¹⁰My child, if sinners entice you, turn your back on them!

¹¹They may say, "Come and join us. Let's hide and kill someone! Just for fun, let's ambush the innocent!

¹²Let's swallow them alive, like the grave; let's swallow them whole, like those who go down to the pit of death.

¹³Think of the great things we'll get! We'll fill our houses with all the stuff we take.

¹⁴Come, throw in your lot with us; we'll all share the loot."

¹⁵My child, don't go along with them! Stay far away from their paths.

¹⁶They rush to commit evil deeds. They hurry to commit murder.

¹⁷If a bird sees a trap being set, it knows to stay away.

¹⁸But these people set an ambush for themselves; they are trying to get themselves killed.

¹⁹Such is the fate of all who are greedy for money; it robs them of life.

²⁰Wisdom shouts in the streets. She cries out in the public square.

²¹She calls to the crowds along the main street, to those gathered in front of the city gate: ²²"How long, you simpletons, will you insist on being simpleminded? How long will you mockers relish your mocking? How long will you fools hate knowledge?

²³Come and listen to my counsel. I'll share my heart with you and make you wise.

²⁴"I called you so often, but you wouldn't come. I reached out to you, but you paid no attention.

²⁵You ignored my advice and rejected the correction I offered.

²⁶So I will laugh when you are in trouble! I will mock you when disaster overtakes you – ²⁷when calamity overtakes you like a storm, when disaster engulfs you like a cyclone, and anguish and distress overwhelm you.

²⁸"When they cry for help, I will not answer. Though they anxiously search for me, they will not find me.

²⁹For they hated knowledge and chose not to fear the Lord.

³⁰They rejected my advice and paid no attention when I corrected them.

³¹Therefore, they must eat the bitter fruit of living their own way, choking on their own schemes.

³²For simpletons turn away from me – to death. Fools are destroyed by their own complacency.

³³But all who listen to me will live in peace, untroubled by fear of harm."

Month One Journal Entry   Date: _____

_____

_____

_____

_____

_____

_____

_____

_____

_____

_____

_____

Month Two Journal Entry   Date: _____

_____

_____

_____

_____

_____

_____

_____

_____

_____

_____

Month Three Journal Entry   Date: _____

_____

_____

_____

_____

_____

_____

_____

_____

_____

Month Four Journal Entry   Date: _____

_____

_____

_____

_____

_____

_____

_____

_____

_____

Month Five Journal Entry   Date: _____

_____

_____

_____

_____

_____

_____

_____

_____

_____

Month Six Journal Entry   Date: _____

_____

_____

_____

_____

_____

_____

_____

_____

_____

_____

Month Seven Journal Entry   Date: _____

_____

_____

_____

_____

_____

_____

_____

_____

_____

Month Eight Journal Entry   Date: _____

_____

_____

_____

_____

_____

_____

_____

_____

_____

Month Nine Journal Entry   Date: _____

_____

_____

_____

_____

_____

_____

_____

_____

_____

_____

Month Ten Journal Entry   Date: _____

_____

_____

_____

_____

_____

_____

_____

_____

_____

_____

Month Eleven Journal Entry   Date: _____

_____

_____

_____

_____

_____

_____

_____

_____

_____

_____

Month Twelve Journal Entry   Date: _____

_____

_____

_____

_____

_____

_____

_____

_____

_____

_____

_____

The Second
Assumptions

"For the Lord gives wisdom; from his mouth come knowledge and understanding. He holds success in store for the upright, he is a shield to those whose walk is blameless, for he guards the course of the just and protects the way of his faithful ones."
~Proverbs 2:6-8 (NIV)

*D*id you see in yesterday's reading that Wisdom is personified in Proverbs 1:20 as female? We read that *she* cries out – in the streets, in the main square – basically wherever there are passers-by. Cries are not soft or muffled statements; when one cries out their voice is raised in effort to be heard.

Wisdom does not sit idly by.

Solomon is telling us that Wisdom is available to everyone, that her desire would be for each of us to be wise. Unfortunately, though the multitudes hear her, there are many who do not heed her call.

Wisdom still cries out today and we see that pursuing her and seeking insight and understanding actually lead us to the knowledge of God. Remember to ask God to unveil truth through the words of this chapter to you - to have His Spirit speak directly to your heart and teach you.

As we read these ancient words, again let us be aware of and put aside any assumptions or preconceived ideas about what this "should" mean. Instead, accept the words written for what they are and consider or meditate on what is truly being said.

A great example of shaking off perceptions comes as we read verses 12 and 14. Verse 12 talks of, "…men whose words are perverse…" and verse 14 speaks of those who, "...rejoice in the perverseness of evil." Many who claim belief in God today have embraced this word to imply something beyond the meaning in the original Hebrew language and even its true definition. The original Hebrew word, "tahpukah", comes from a root word meaning "to turn about or over" (Strong's Exhaustive Bible Concordance). It is also defined as FROward (as in when we are tossed to and fro). In other words, a perverse person is a fraud and they cannot represent truth, for they come from a place of internal chaos and disharmony.

Carried forward to today, we should understand that perverse people are those whose words, decisions and actions have no solid foundation and they often take pride in being oppositional. Their self-interest blinds them to true justice, equity, righteousness, mercy and all good things. Let's do our best to drop any preconceived notions we may have about what Solomon is saying when he uses this word and embrace its true definition whenever we see it mentioned as we read through Proverbs.

Proverbs Chapter 2
(NIV)

¹My son, if you accept my words and store up my commands within you, ²turning your ear to wisdom and applying your heart to understanding – ³indeed, if you call out for insight and cry aloud for understanding, ⁴and if you look for it as for silver and search for it as for hidden treasure, ⁵then you will understand the fear of the Lord and find the knowledge of God.

⁶For the Lord gives wisdom; from his mouth come knowledge and understanding.

⁷He holds success in store for the upright, he is a shield to those whose walk is blameless, ⁸for he guards the course of the just and protects the way of his faithful ones.

⁹Then you will understand what is right and just and fair – every good path.

¹⁰For wisdom will enter your heart, and knowledge will be pleasant to your soul.

¹¹Discretion will protect you, and understanding will guard you.

¹²Wisdom will save you from the ways of wicked men, from men whose words are perverse, ¹³who have left the straight paths to walk in dark ways, ¹⁴who delight in doing wrong and rejoice in the perverseness of evil, ¹⁵whose paths are crooked and who are devious in their ways.

¹⁶Wisdom will save you also from the adulterous woman, from the wayward woman with her seductive words, ¹⁷who has left the partner of her youth and ignored the covenant she made before God.

¹⁸Surely her house leads down to death and her paths to the spirits of the dead.

¹⁹None who go to her return or attain the paths of life.

²⁰Thus you will walk in the ways of the good and keep to the paths of the righteous.

²¹For the upright will live in the land, and the blameless will remain in it; ²²but the wicked will be cut off from the land, and the unfaithful will be torn from it.

Month One Journal Entry   Date: _____

_____

_____

_____

_____

_____

_____

_____

_____

_____

_____

Month Two Journal Entry   Date: _____

_____

_____

_____

_____

_____

_____

_____

_____

_____

_____

_____

Month Three Journal Entry   Date: _____

_____
_____
_____
_____
_____
_____
_____
_____
_____
_____

Month Four Journal Entry   Date: _____

_____
_____
_____
_____
_____
_____
_____
_____
_____
_____

Month Five Journal Entry   Date: _____

_____
_____
_____
_____
_____
_____
_____
_____
_____
_____

Month Six Journal Entry   Date: _____

_____
_____
_____
_____
_____
_____
_____
_____
_____
_____
_____

Month Seven Journal Entry   Date: _____

_____
_____
_____
_____
_____
_____
_____
_____
_____
_____

Month Eight Journal Entry   Date: _____

_____
_____
_____
_____
_____
_____
_____
_____
_____
_____

Month Nine Journal Entry   Date: _____

_____

_____

_____

_____

_____

_____

_____

_____

_____

Month Ten Journal Entry   Date: _____

_____

_____

_____

_____

_____

_____

_____

_____

_____

_____

Month Eleven Journal Entry   Date: _____

_____

_____

_____

_____

_____

_____

_____

_____

_____

_____

Month Twelve Journal Entry   Date: _____

_____

_____

_____

_____

_____

_____

_____

_____

_____

_____

The Third

Identity

*"How blessed is the man who finds wisdom and the man who gains understanding.
For her profit is better than the profit of silver and her gain better than fine gold.
She is more precious than jewels; and nothing you desire compares with her."*
~Proverbs 3:13-15 (NASB)

*T*oday we again see the chapter opening with the words, "My son." Spoken lovingly as from parent to child, the words are meant to build us up inside, to strengthen that part of us that must be steady in turbulent times, when indecision and external factors would sway us and have us doubt our identity, and when they would steer us from our God-given destinies.

Verse 3 tells us to bind kindness and truth around our necks, to write them on the tablets of our hearts. Think about that for a moment. Kindness and truth are not to be subject to how we feel. They are to be hallmarks of who we are, and verse 4 tells us we will find great results if we persevere: we would find favor and a good reputation first in the sight of God, but also in the sight of man. Which one of us wouldn't desire these good things?

Reproof, as we see in verse 12, is correction for a fault. We see this word throughout Scripture. Just as parents correct the children they love, so God will allow corrective action to come into our lives because He loves us. Yes, He blesses us, but He also corrects us, that we would be aligned more with His characteristics and His righteousness.

This fantastic, expansive universe we dwell within was created with intention, with thought, with understanding and awareness. Verses 19-20 teach us that wisdom, understanding and knowledge all were instrumental in the creation of the world. Are we using these principles to build up and into the world around us, to fulfill our unique destinies? Perhaps you have thought of these principles as boring, but truly *look* at the natural world around you – the landscapes, the delicate yet strong balance of animals, insects, flora and fauna. How beautiful it all is! Ephesians 5:1 tells us we should be dear children who live as imitators of our Father. How different could our lives be if we consistently built and created from a place of wisdom, understanding and knowledge?

Proverbs Chapter 3
(NASB)

¹My son, do not forget my teaching, but let your heart keep my commandments; ²for length of days and years of life and peace they will add to you.

³Do not let kindness and truth leave you; bind them around your neck, write them on the tablet of your heart.

⁴So you will find favor and good repute in the sight of God and man.

⁵Trust in the Lord with all your heart and do not lean on your own understanding.

⁶In all your ways acknowledge Him, and He will make your paths straight.

⁷Do not be wise in your own eyes; fear the Lord and turn away from evil.

⁸It will be healing to your body and refreshment to your bones.

⁹Honor the Lord from your wealth and from the first of all your produce; ¹⁰so your barns will be filled with plenty and your vats will overflow with new wine.

¹¹My son, do not reject the discipline of the Lord or loathe His reproof, ¹²for whom the Lord loves He reproves, even as a father corrects the son in whom he delights.

¹³How blessed is the man who finds wisdom and the man who gains understanding.

¹⁴For her profit is better than the profit of silver and her gain better than fine gold.

¹⁵She is more precious than jewels; and nothing you desire compares with her.

¹⁶Long life is in her right hand; in her left hand are riches and honor.

¹⁷Her ways are pleasant ways and all her paths are peace.

¹⁸She is a tree of life to those who take hold of her, and happy are all who hold her fast.

¹⁹The Lord by wisdom founded the earth, by understanding He established the heavens.

²⁰By His knowledge the deeps were broken up and the skies drip with dew.

²¹My son, let them not vanish from your sight; keep sound wisdom and discretion, ²²so they will be life to your soul and adornment to your neck.

²³Then you will walk in your way securely and your foot will not stumble.

²⁴When you lie down, you will not be afraid; when you lie down, your sleep will be sweet.

²⁵Do not be afraid of sudden fear nor of the onslaught of the wicked when it comes; ²⁶for the Lord will be your confidence and will keep your foot from being caught.

²⁷Do not withhold good from those to whom it is due, when it is in your power to do it.

²⁸Do not say to your neighbor, "Go, and come back, and tomorrow I will give it," when you have it with you.

²⁹Do not devise harm against your neighbor, while he lives securely beside you.

³⁰Do not contend with a man without cause, if he has done you no harm.

³¹Do not envy a man of violence and do not choose any of his ways.

³²For the devious are an abomination to the Lord; but He is intimate with the upright.

³³The curse of the Lord is on the house of the wicked, but He blesses the dwelling of the righteous.

³⁴Though He scoffs at the scoffers, yet He gives grace to the afflicted.

³⁵The wise will inherit honor, but fools display dishonor.

Month One Journal Entry   Date: _____

_____

_____

_____

_____

_____

_____

_____

_____

_____

_____

Month Two Journal Entry   Date: _____

_____

_____

_____

_____

_____

_____

_____

_____

_____

_____

_____

Month Three Journal Entry   Date: _____

_____

_____

_____

_____

_____

_____

_____

_____

_____

Month Four Journal Entry   Date: _____

_____

_____

_____

_____

_____

_____

_____

_____

_____

Month Five Journal Entry   Date: _____

_____

_____

_____

_____

_____

_____

_____

_____

_____

_____

Month Six Journal Entry   Date: _____

_____

_____

_____

_____

_____

_____

_____

_____

_____

_____

Month Seven Journal Entry   Date: _____

_____

_____

_____

_____

_____

_____

_____

_____

_____

Month Eight Journal Entry   Date: _____

_____

_____

_____

_____

_____

_____

_____

_____

_____

Month Nine Journal Entry   Date: _____

_____
_____
_____
_____
_____
_____
_____
_____
_____
_____

Month Ten Journal Entry   Date: _____

_____
_____
_____
_____
_____
_____
_____
_____
_____
_____

Month Eleven Journal Entry   Date: _____

_____
_____
_____
_____
_____
_____
_____
_____
_____

Month Twelve Journal Entry   Date: _____

_____
_____
_____
_____
_____
_____
_____
_____
_____

The Fourth
Diligence

"The beginning of wisdom is: Acquire wisdom; And with all your acquiring, get understanding."
~Proverbs 4:7 (NASB)

*J*ust get it done. That's what Solomon is telling us here. You must acquire wisdom to be a wise person, so just get started. Do more than acquire words of wisdom, but also set our hearts to gain understanding so that we would practice and apply wisdom's principles in our lives. We may be a little wobbly at first as we work this out in our lives, but God is with us and for us. He will guide us and He will bless us for our desire to be a person of wisdom. Remember what James says, *"If any of you lacks wisdom, you should ask God, who gives generously to all without finding fault, and it will be given to you."(James 1:5, NIV)*

A continued practice in wisdom changes us from the inside out. We shall have new and improved responses to others as well as to the situations we encounter in life. Wisdom will ultimately change our heart, our perceptions, and our actions.

Today, in fact, we are instructed to, *"Watch over your heart with all diligence, for from it flow the springs of life,"* *(Proverbs 4:23, NASB)*. It's our sacred duty to diligently watch over our own hearts. We cannot pawn our hearts out to others to care for – they are ours to guard. The Hebrew word for diligence actually implies a place of confinement, like a prison. Yes, we are to guard our hearts with the diligence of a prison guard over prisoners. Guards in some ancient cultures would be put to death if their prisoners escaped, so this point was not taken lightly when it was penned.

Ultimately, what we've allowed into our hearts will not just remain dormant. It will grow in strength until it overflows to the world around us and will impact the legacy we impart – whether for good or harm.

What do you choose to allow into your heart? I only want wisdom, joy, life, love, harmony, compassion and good springing from me. The legacy I leave will echo to my generations by what I allow in.

Let us set our guard, remain focused, and never waver.

Proverbs Chapter 4
(NASB)

[1]Hear, O sons, the instruction of a father, and give attention that you may gain understanding, [2]for I give you sound teaching; do not abandon my instruction.

[3]When I was a son to my father, tender and the only son in the sight of my mother, [4]then he taught me and said to me, "Let your heart hold fast my words; keep my commandments and live; [5]acquire wisdom! Acquire understanding! Do not forget nor turn away from the words of my mouth.

[6]"Do not forsake her, and she will guard you; love her, and she will watch over you.

[7]"The beginning of wisdom is: Acquire wisdom; and with all your acquiring, get understanding.

[8]"Prize her, and she will exalt you; she will honor you if you embrace her.

[9]"She will place on your head a garland of grace; she will present you with a crown of beauty.

[10]Hear, my son, and accept my sayings and the years of your life will be many.

[11]I have directed you in the way of wisdom; I have led you in upright paths.

[12]When you walk, your steps will not be impeded; and if you run, you will not stumble.

[13]Take hold of instruction; do not let go. Guard her, for she is your life.

[14]Do not enter the path of the wicked and do not proceed in the way of evil men.

[15]Avoid it, do not pass by it; turn away from it and pass on.

[16]For they cannot sleep unless they do evil; and they are robbed of sleep unless they make someone stumble.

[17]For they eat the bread of wickedness and drink the wine of violence.

[18]But the path of the righteous is like the light of dawn, that shines brighter and brighter until the full day.

[19]The way of the wicked is like darkness; they do not know over what they stumble.

[20]My son, give attention to my words; incline your ear to my sayings.

²¹Do not let them depart from your sight; keep them in the midst of your heart.

²²For they are life to those who find them and health to all their body.

²³Watch over your heart with all diligence, for from it flow the springs of life.

²⁴Put away from you a deceitful mouth and put devious speech far from you.

²⁵Let your eyes look directly ahead and let your gaze be fixed straight in front of you.

²⁶Watch the path of your feet and all your ways will be established.

²⁷Do not turn to the right nor to the left; turn your foot from evil.

Month One Journal Entry   Date: _____

_____

_____

_____

_____

_____

_____

_____

_____

_____

_____

Month Two Journal Entry   Date: _____

_____

_____

_____

_____

_____

_____

_____

_____

_____

_____

Month Three Journal Entry   Date: _____

_____
_____
_____
_____
_____
_____
_____
_____
_____
_____
_____
_____

Month Four Journal Entry   Date: _____

_____
_____
_____
_____
_____
_____
_____
_____
_____
_____
_____
_____

Month Five Journal Entry   Date: _____

_____
_____
_____
_____
_____
_____
_____
_____
_____

Month Six Journal Entry   Date: _____

_____
_____
_____
_____
_____
_____
_____
_____
_____
_____
_____
_____

Month Seven Journal Entry   Date: _____

_____

_____

_____

_____

_____

_____

_____

_____

_____

Month Eight Journal Entry   Date: _____

_____

_____

_____

_____

_____

_____

_____

_____

_____

Month Nine Journal Entry   Date: _____

_____

_____

_____

_____

_____

_____

_____

_____

_____

_____

_____

Month Ten Journal Entry   Date: _____

_____

_____

_____

_____

_____

_____

_____

_____

_____

_____

_____

Month Eleven Journal Entry   Date: _____

_____

_____

_____

_____

_____

_____

_____

_____

_____

_____

Month Twelve Journal Entry   Date: _____

_____

_____

_____

_____

_____

_____

_____

_____

_____

_____

The Fifth
The Core

"My son, pay attention to my wisdom; listen carefully to my wise counsel. Then you will show discernment, and your lips will express what you've learned."
~Proverbs 5:1-2 (NLT)

Today, look beyond just the images conveyed by the words to the central truth of what Solomon is saying in Proverbs 5.

What are we building our inner spiritual man, our very core, on?

Proverbs 23:7 tells us that as a man thinks in his heart, so he is.

Remember the Hebrew meaning of diligence that we discussed yesterday? What we are diligent to focus on–wisdom or folly, truth or opinion, lack or abundance–becomes part of who we are.

Notice the process described in the first two verses of this proverb: verse 1 tells us to pay attention to wisdom and listen carefully to wise counsel, and verse 2 gives us the outcome – then you will show discernment and your lips will express what you've learned.

This truth Solomon shares is that we must surround ourselves with wisdom and pay attention to it. There is a process here that requires we go beyond just hearing to listening and absorbing. The process shall work for good in our lives, to strengthen and build us up at our core.

The opposite is also true: surround ourselves with negativity, with pride, with foolishness, pay attention to those and listen carefully to the words of those who profess those opinions, and the process will still work in us. We will build a foundation based on faulty, unstable characteristics.

Hear the story Proverbs 5 tells today. It speaks of the core characteristics of one who would choose to lead others astray, and one who would choose to be led astray. Both have a choice to follow wisdom's guidance or temporary pleasure. One cares nothing about the path to life, the other finds themselves filled with regret.

Our conclusion should be to study wisdom, saturate ourselves with wisdom at our core, seek and desire it, and then our instincts and actions will be to follow wisdom's path.

Proverbs Chapter 5
(NLT)

[1]My son, pay attention to my wisdom; listen carefully to my wise counsel.

[2]Then you will show discernment, and your lips will express what you've learned.

[3]For the lips of an immoral woman are as sweet as honey, and her mouth is smoother than oil.

[4]But in the end she is as bitter as poison, as dangerous as a double-edged sword.

[5]Her feet go down to death; her steps lead straight to the grave.

[6]For she cares nothing about the path to life. She staggers down a crooked trail and doesn't realize it.

[7]So now, my sons, listen to me. Never stray from what I am about to say: [8]Stay away from her! Don't go near the door of her house!

[9]If you do, you will lose your honor and will lose to merciless people all you have achieved.

[10]Strangers will consume your wealth, and someone else will enjoy the fruit of your labor.

[11]In the end you will groan in anguish when disease consumes your body.

[12]You will say, "How I hated discipline! If only I had not ignored all the warnings!

[13]Oh, why didn't I listen to my teachers? Why didn't I pay attention to my instructors?

[14]I have come to the brink of utter ruin, and now I must face public disgrace."

[15]Drink water from your own well – share your love only with your wife.

[16]Why spill the water of your springs in the streets, having sex with just anyone?

[17]You should reserve it for yourselves. Never share it with strangers.

[18]Let your wife be a fountain of blessing for you. Rejoice in the wife of your youth.

[19]She is a loving deer, a graceful doe. Let her breasts satisfy you always. May you always be captivated by her love.

²⁰Why be captivated, my son, by an immoral woman, or fondle the breasts of a promiscuous woman?

²¹For the Lord sees clearly what a man does, examining every path he takes.

²²An evil man is held captive by his own sins; they are ropes that catch and hold him.

²³He will die for lack of self-control; he will be lost because of his great foolishness.

Month One Journal Entry   Date: _____

_____

_____

_____

_____

_____

_____

_____

_____

_____

Month Two Journal Entry   Date: _____

_____

_____

_____

_____

_____

_____

_____

_____

_____

Month Three Journal Entry   Date: _____

_____

_____

_____

_____

_____

_____

_____

_____

_____

Month Four Journal Entry   Date: _____

_____

_____

_____

_____

_____

_____

_____

_____

_____

_____

Month Five Journal Entry   Date: _____

_____

_____

_____

_____

_____

_____

_____

_____

_____

Month Six Journal Entry   Date: _____

_____

_____

_____

_____

_____

_____

_____

_____

_____

_____

Month Seven Journal Entry   Date: _____

_____

_____

_____

_____

_____

_____

_____

_____

_____

_____

Month Eight Journal Entry   Date: _____

_____

_____

_____

_____

_____

_____

_____

_____

_____

_____

Month Nine Journal Entry   Date: _____

_____

_____

_____

_____

_____

_____

_____

_____

_____

Month Ten Journal Entry   Date: _____

_____

_____

_____

_____

_____

_____

_____

_____

_____

Month Eleven Journal Entry   Date: _____

_____

_____

_____

_____

_____

_____

_____

_____

_____

Month Twelve Journal Entry   Date: _____

_____

_____

_____

_____

_____

_____

_____

_____

_____

The Sixth

Freedom

"For this command is a lamp, this teaching is a light, and correction and instruction
are the way to life..."
~Proverbs 6:23 (NIV)

Today we read of having an awareness of our individual freedom. It is something to be cherished, and not taken lightly.

Solomon tells us in verse 3 that if we have become a guarantor for a friend's debt – if we have committed something we have worked for to be subject to the hands of another - we should free ourselves like a gazelle fights to flee from the hunter's hand or fowler's trap. We should give our neighbor no rest until we have freed ourselves. Why would he say this?

We have sacrificed our God-given freedom to the actions of someone else.

Freedom is more than doing what feels good to us. There is responsibility involved. Look at the tiny ant – it knows perfectly and instinctively its high calling to fulfill its role in the colony. Yet how many of us defy the voice of the Spirit within and set about to fulfill selfish desires when we have a destiny calling?

We push back against the higher calling of God to satisfy the opinions of people or what are ultimately passing pleasures, trading destiny for momentary ease. Freedom dwells, though, at that higher calling from God unique to each of us, the calling that requires intentional action, the calling planted within, that speaks to our heart, that will benefit others as well as ourselves.

Verses 16 through 19 tell us seven things God hates and finds detestable. If God finds these detestable, His Spirit that dwells in us will find these detestable, too, so let's really pay attention to these today. They may surprise you. They are not about religious activity, telling people what is right and wrong, how to live by external rules or politically correct statements. They all boil down to matters of our true nature - behaviors that may emanate from a core that is not aligned with His will; therefore, they do not impact the world for good. Read this passage to understand what He detests and then use wisdom to understand the opposite - what pleases Him.

Consider writing in your journal today the opposite of everything He hates, that you may have insight and guidance in how to live wisely.

Proverbs Chapter 6
(NIV)

¹My son, if you have put up security for your neighbor, if you have shaken hands in pledge for a stranger, ²you have been trapped by what you said, ensnared by the words of your mouth.

³So do this, my son, to free yourself, since you have fallen into your neighbor's hands: Go – to the point of exhaustion – and give your neighbor no rest!

⁴Allow no sleep to your eyes, no slumber to your eyelids.

⁵Free yourself, like a gazelle from the hand of the hunter, like a bird from the snare of the fowler.

⁶Go to the ant, you sluggard; consider its ways and be wise!

⁷It has no commander, no overseer or ruler, ⁸yet it stores its provisions in summer and gathers its food at harvest.

⁹How long will you lie there, you sluggard? When will you get up from your sleep?

¹⁰A little sleep, a little slumber, a little folding of the hands to rest – and poverty will come on you like a thief and scarcity like an armed man.

¹²A troublemaker and a villain, who goes about with a corrupt mouth, ¹³who winks maliciously with his eye, signals with his feet and motions with his fingers, ¹⁴who plots evil with deceit in his heart – he always stirs up conflict.

¹⁵Therefore disaster will overtake him in an instant; he will suddenly be destroyed – without remedy.

¹⁶There are six things the Lord hates, seven that are detestable to him: ¹⁷haughty eyes, a lying tongue, hands that shed innocent blood, ¹⁸a heart that devises wicked schemes, feet that are quick to rush into evil, ¹⁹a false witness who pours out lies and a person who stirs up conflict in the community.

²⁰My son, keep your father's command and do not forsake your mother's teaching.

²¹Bind them always on your heart; fasten them around your neck.

²²When you walk, they will guide you; when you sleep, they will watch over you; when you awake, they will speak to you.

²³For this command is a lamp, this teaching is a light, and correction and instruction are the way to life, ²⁴keeping you from your neighbor's wife, from the smooth talk of a wayward woman.

²⁵Do not lust in your heart after her beauty or let her captivate you with her eyes.

²⁶For a prostitute can be had for a loaf of bread, but another man's wife preys on your very life.

²⁷Can a man scoop fire into his lap without his clothes being burned?

²⁸Can a man walk on hot coals without his feet being scorched?

²⁹So is he who sleeps with another man's wife; no one who touches her will go unpunished.

³⁰People do not despise a thief if he steals to satisfy his hunger when he is starving.

³¹Yet if he is caught, he must pay sevenfold, though it costs him all the wealth of his house.

³²But a man who commits adultery has no sense; whoever does so destroys himself.

³³Blows and disgrace are his lot, and his shame will never be wiped away.

³⁴For jealousy arouses a husband's fury, and he will show no mercy when he takes revenge.

³⁵He will not accept any compensation; he will refuse a bribe, however great it is.

Month One Journal Entry   Date: _____

_____

_____

_____

_____

_____

_____

_____

_____

_____

Month Two Journal Entry   Date: _____

_____

_____

_____

_____

_____

_____

_____

_____

_____

Month Three Journal Entry   Date: _____

_____
_____
_____
_____
_____
_____
_____
_____
_____
_____

Month Four Journal Entry   Date: _____

_____
_____
_____
_____
_____
_____
_____
_____
_____
_____

Month Five Journal Entry   Date: _____

_____

_____

_____

_____

_____

_____

_____

_____

_____

_____

Month Six Journal Entry   Date: _____

_____

_____

_____

_____

_____

_____

_____

_____

_____

_____

_____

Month Seven Journal Entry   Date: _____

_____
_____
_____
_____
_____
_____
_____
_____
_____
_____

Month Eight Journal Entry   Date: _____

_____
_____
_____
_____
_____
_____
_____
_____
_____
_____

Month Nine Journal Entry   Date: _____

_____

_____

_____

_____

_____

_____

_____

_____

_____

Month Ten Journal Entry   Date: _____

_____

_____

_____

_____

_____

_____

_____

_____

_____

_____

Month Eleven Journal Entry   Date: _____

_____

_____

_____

_____

_____

_____

_____

_____

_____

_____

Month Twelve Journal Entry   Date: _____

_____

_____

_____

_____

_____

_____

_____

_____

_____

_____

_____

The Seventh
The Will

"Love wisdom like a sister; make insight a beloved member of your family."
~Proverbs 7:4 (NLT)

Today's reading is basically a study in cause and effect. There are two main characters we read about and they demonstrate the downward spiral we face when wisdom is cast aside. We read that the woman is the "brash, rebellious" type. In the original Hebrew language, "brash" implies being in great commotion or tumult. This woman may appear beautiful and delightfully seductive, but her heart is full of chaos.

A heart full of chaos will reflect chaos in a person's actions. Proverbs 4:23 told us that from the heart flow the springs of life; therefore, if chaos is at the heart, chaos will flow in what springs forth from our lives. That's definitely something to consider.

The young man, we read, lacks common sense. Turning again to the original language, we see that the term for "sense" is also used for the will and the intellect. Every human being has the higher powers of the will and intellect. It's our role to actively grow and sharpen these powers. This man was not relegated by God to a life lacking common sense. He had the same opportunity you and I do to gain insight and wisdom, to use his will to choose to develop his mind and awareness, that he would heed the voice of God telling him to stay on his side of the street. He was not destined to cross the street and walk past the house of the seductress – it was a choice made from unenlightened free will.

Note that: unenlightened free will. God has granted us all the precious gift of free will, and He honors our ability to choose, even when our choices aren't wise. Choosing what feels good versus what's best for our higher calling often connects us to people or behaviors that entrap us. This is just one of the reasons why the *practice* of wisdom is so important. Diligently filling our minds with wise words, with God's knowledge and insight, enlightens our free will, illuminating the potential errors of our ways, empowering us to live in alignment with God's order and to keep to the right side of the street.

We so clearly see the collision of two people living outside of the right order of things in this chapter, two very different people who will meet and likely create ripples of more disorder between them, for chaos + chaos can only equal more chaos. Order will not naturally flow from chaos.

This wisdom Solomon writes of endured for thousands of years before he was born and is still true thousands of years later. Let us hold fast to growing in wisdom, insight & understanding. They will always profit us and direct us toward our highest calling.

Proverbs Chapter 7
(NLT)

[1]Follow my advice, my son; always treasure my commands.

[2]Obey my commands and live! Guard my instructions as you guard your own eyes.

[3]Tie them on your fingers as a reminder. Write them deep within your heart.

[4]Love wisdom like a sister; make insight a beloved member of your family.

[5]Let them protect you from an affair with an immoral woman, from listening to the flattery of a promiscuous woman.

[6]While I was at the window of my house, looking through the curtain, [7]I saw some naïve young men, and one in particular who lacked common sense.

[8]He was crossing the street near the house of an immoral woman, strolling down the path by her house.

[9]It was at twilight, in the evening, as deep darkness fell.

[10]The woman approached him, seductively dressed and sly of heart.

[11]She was the brash, rebellious type, never content to stay at home.

[12]She is often in the streets and markets, soliciting at every corner.

[13]She threw her arms around him and kissed him, and with a brazen look she said, [14]"I've just made my peace offerings and fulfilled my vows.

[15]You're the one I was looking for! I came out to find you, and here you are!

[16]My bed is spread with beautiful blankets, with colored sheets of Egyptian linen.

[17]I've perfumed my bed with myrrh, aloes, and cinnamon.

[18]Come, let's drink our fill of love until morning. Let's enjoy each other's caresses, [19]for my husband is not home. He's away on a long trip.

[20]He has taken a wallet full of money with him and won't return until later this month."

[21]So she seduced him with her pretty speech and enticed him with her flattery.

[22]He followed her at once, like an ox going to the slaughter. He was like a stag caught in a trap, [23]awaiting the arrow that would pierce its heart. He was like a bird flying into a snare, little knowing it would cost him his life.

[24]So listen to me, my sons, and pay attention to my words.

[25]Don't let your hearts stray away toward her. Don't wander down her wayward path.

[26]For she has been the ruin of many; many men have been her victims.

[27]Her house is the road to the grave. Her bedroom is the den of death.

Month One Journal Entry   Date: _____

_____

_____

_____

_____

_____

_____

_____

_____

_____

_____

Month Two Journal Entry   Date: _____

_____

_____

_____

_____

_____

_____

_____

_____

_____

_____

Month Three Journal Entry   Date: _____

_____

_____

_____

_____

_____

_____

_____

_____

_____

_____

Month Four Journal Entry   Date: _____

_____

_____

_____

_____

_____

_____

_____

_____

_____

_____

_____

Month Five Journal Entry   Date: _____

_____

_____

_____

_____

_____

_____

_____

_____

_____

_____

Month Six Journal Entry   Date: _____

_____

_____

_____

_____

_____

_____

_____

_____

_____

_____

Month Seven Journal Entry   Date: _____

_____

_____

_____

_____

_____

_____

_____

_____

_____

Month Eight Journal Entry   Date: _____

_____

_____

_____

_____

_____

_____

_____

_____

_____

_____

Month Nine Journal Entry   Date: _____

_____

_____

_____

_____

_____

_____

_____

_____

_____

Month Ten Journal Entry   Date: _____

_____

_____

_____

_____

_____

_____

_____

_____

_____

Month Eleven Journal Entry   Date: _____

_____

_____

_____

_____

_____

_____

_____

_____

_____

_____

Month Twelve Journal Entry   Date: _____

_____

_____

_____

_____

_____

_____

_____

_____

_____

_____

_____

_____

_____

The Eighth
Precision

"Common sense and success belong to me. Insight and strength are mine."
~Proverbs 8:14 (NLT)

Wisdom takes the microphone today, and she speaks ever so eloquently. Verses 4 through 36 are Wisdom's words, testifying to us. As an attribute of God, she speaks as He does: precisely, never wasting a word.

I love that God never wastes words when He speaks in Scripture. His words are always truth, clothed in righteousness, and never dully repetitive like the words people often speak. He gets right to the heart of a matter and doesn't indulge needless conversation or point out useless things. Every single word He says matters.

Wisdom tells us she stands on a hilltop at the crossroads and that she stands at the entrance to the town. Think about those positions: she is out in public places, where all would hear her. She is not hidden away in a corner of the sanctuary or buried under the rocks of an altar. There is no secret map needed to find her. She makes herself available in the populated areas where she would reach many because she has important topics to address:

Truth.
Instruction.
Gifts.

How she was formed by God from the beginning – giving us insight into steps of creation, rejoicing with the human family. How beautiful, that she would celebrate joyfully with us!

Hear what Wisdom has to say about herself today and how she wishes to pour into us. Practice the knowledge of Wisdom daily, embrace her, infuse your life with her.

"And how happy I was with the world he created; how I rejoiced with the human family!"
~Wisdom speaking in Proverbs 8:31 (NLT)

Proverbs Chapter 8
(NLT)

¹Listen as Wisdom calls out! Hear as understanding raises her voice!

²On the hilltop along the road, she takes her stand at the crossroads.

³By the gates at the entrance to the town, on the road leading in, she cries aloud, ⁴"I call to you, to all of you! I raise my voice to all people.

⁵You simple people, use good judgment. You foolish people, show some understanding.

⁶Listen to me! For I have important things to tell you. Everything I say is right, ⁷for I speak the truth and detest every kind of deception.

⁸My advice is wholesome. There is nothing devious or crooked in it.

⁹My words are plain to anyone with understanding, clear to those with knowledge.

¹⁰Choose my instruction rather than silver, and knowledge rather than pure gold.

¹¹For wisdom is far more valuable than rubies. Nothing you desire can compare with it.

¹²"I, Wisdom, live together with good judgment. I know where to discover knowledge and discernment.

¹³All who fear the Lord will hate evil. Therefore, I hate pride and arrogance, corruption and perverse speech.

¹⁴Common sense and success belong to me. Insight and strength are mine.

¹⁵Because of me, kings reign, and rulers make just decrees.

¹⁶Rulers lead with my help, and nobles make righteous judgments.

¹⁷"I love all who love me. Those who search will surely find me.

¹⁸I have riches and honor, as well as enduring wealth and justice.

¹⁹My gifts are better than gold, even the purest gold, my wages better than sterling silver!

²⁰I walk in righteousness, in paths of justice.

[21]Those who love me inherit wealth. I will fill their treasuries.

[22]"The Lord formed me from the beginning, before he created anything else.

[23]I was appointed in ages past, at the very first, before the earth began.

[24]I was born before the oceans were created, before the springs bubbled forth their waters.

[25]Before the mountains were formed, before the hills, I was born – [26]before he had made the earth and fields and first handfuls of soil.

[27]I was there when he established the heavens, when he drew the horizon on the oceans.

[28]I was there when he set the clouds above, when he established springs deep in the earth.

[29]I was there when he set the limits of the seas, so they would not spread beyond their boundaries. And when he marked off the earth's foundations, [30]I was the architect at his side.

I was his constant delight, rejoicing always in his presence.

[31]And how happy I was with the world he created; how I rejoiced with the human family!

[32]"And so, my children, listen to me, for all who follow my ways are joyful.

[33]Listen to my instruction and be wise. Don't ignore it.

[34]Joyful are those who listen to me, watching for me daily at my gates, waiting for me outside my home!

[35]For whoever finds me finds life and receives favor from the Lord.

[36]But those who miss me injure themselves. All who hate me love death."

Month One Journal Entry   Date: _____

_____

_____

_____

_____

_____

_____

_____

_____

_____

_____

_____

Month Two Journal Entry   Date: _____

_____

_____

_____

_____

_____

_____

_____

_____

_____

_____

_____

Month Three Journal Entry   Date: _____

_____

_____

_____

_____

_____

_____

_____

_____

_____

_____

Month Four Journal Entry   Date: _____

_____

_____

_____

_____

_____

_____

_____

_____

_____

_____

_____

Month Five Journal Entry   Date: _____

_____

_____

_____

_____

_____

_____

_____

_____

_____

Month Six Journal Entry   Date: _____

_____

_____

_____

_____

_____

_____

_____

_____

_____

Month Seven Journal Entry   Date: _____

_____
_____
_____
_____
_____
_____
_____
_____
_____
_____

Month Eight Journal Entry   Date: _____

_____
_____
_____
_____
_____
_____
_____
_____
_____

Month Nine Journal Entry   Date: _____

_____

_____

_____

_____

_____

_____

_____

_____

_____

_____

Month Ten Journal Entry   Date: _____

_____

_____

_____

_____

_____

_____

_____

_____

_____

_____

Month Eleven Journal Entry   Date: _____

_____

_____

_____

_____

_____

_____

_____

_____

_____

_____

Month Twelve Journal Entry   Date: _____

_____

_____

_____

_____

_____

_____

_____

_____

_____

_____

The Ninth

Invitation

"For through wisdom your days will be many, and years will be added to your life."
~Proverbs 9:11 (NIV)

What wonderful promises we discover today!

- Through wisdom our days will be many
- Years will be added to our lives
- Our application of wisdom shall reward us, if we are wise

We see two houses described in Proverbs 9: Wisdom's house and the house of the unruly. Notice again how Wisdom calls from the highest points of the city, inviting people to her house. I picture her as a silver-haired woman of grace, arms open to receive and usher in guests. She is available to everyone and, in fact, is reaching out specifically to the simple.

Contrast Wisdom's invitation with that of the unruly woman. The unruly woman mimics Wisdom as she also calls out to those who pass by. There are differences, though. Notice her posture–that alone speaks volumes. The Hebrew word here for unruly implies to be in commotion or tumult. We've seen that before, right? Yes, the house of the unruly woman is the house of chaos.

The unruly woman also speaks to the simple, and that gives us the glorious insight into our Father's love for mankind. He does not allow just the foolish woman to call out to the simple, He already has Wisdom poised, also calling to them, beseeching them to pursue her. We see His heart to love justly, with equity – His desire is that all have the opportunity to gain Wisdom's treasures.

As you read Proverbs 9, consider what is gained (or lost) by those who enter each dwelling place.

Proverbs Chapter 9
(NIV)

[1]Wisdom has built her house. She has set up its seven pillars.

[2]She has prepared her meat and mixed her wine; she has also set her table.

[3]She has sent out her servants, and she calls from the highest point of the city, [4]"Let all who are simple come to my house!" To those who have no sense she says, [5]"Come, eat my food and drink the wine I have mixed.

[6]Leave your simple ways and you will live; walk in the way of insight."

[7]Whoever corrects a mocker invites insults; whoever rebukes the wicked incurs abuse.

[8]Do not rebuke mockers or they will hate you; rebuke the wise and they will love you.

[9]Instruct the wise and they will be wiser still; teach the righteous and they will add to their learning.

[10]The fear of the Lord is the beginning of wisdom, and knowledge of the Holy One is understanding.

[11]For through wisdom your days will be many, and years will be added to your life.

[12]If you are wise, your wisdom will reward you; if you are a mocker, you alone will suffer.

[13]Folly is an unruly woman; she is simple and knows nothing.

[14]She sits at the door of her house, on a seat at the highest point of the city, [15]calling out to those who pass by, who go straight on their way, [16]"Let all who are simple come to my house!"

To those who have no sense she says, [17]"Stolen water is sweet; food eaten in secret is delicious!"

[18]But little do they know that the dead are there, that her guests are deep in the realm of the dead.

Month One Journal Entry   Date: _____

_____
_____
_____
_____
_____
_____
_____
_____
_____
_____
_____

Month Two Journal Entry   Date: _____

_____
_____
_____
_____
_____
_____
_____
_____
_____
_____
_____

Month Three Journal Entry   Date: _____

_____

_____

_____

_____

_____

_____

_____

_____

_____

_____

Month Four Journal Entry   Date: _____

_____

_____

_____

_____

_____

_____

_____

_____

_____

_____

Month Five Journal Entry   Date: _____

_____

_____

_____

_____

_____

_____

_____

_____

Month Six Journal Entry   Date: _____

_____

_____

_____

_____

_____

_____

_____

_____

_____

Month Seven Journal Entry   Date: _____

_____
_____
_____
_____
_____
_____
_____
_____
_____

Month Eight Journal Entry   Date: _____

_____
_____
_____
_____
_____
_____
_____
_____
_____
_____

Month Nine Journal Entry   Date: _____

_____

_____

_____

_____

_____

_____

_____

_____

_____

_____

_____

Month Ten Journal Entry   Date: _____

_____

_____

_____

_____

_____

_____

_____

_____

_____

_____

_____

Month Eleven Journal Entry   Date: _____

_____

_____

_____

_____

_____

_____

_____

_____

_____

_____

Month Twelve Journal Entry   Date: _____

_____

_____

_____

_____

_____

_____

_____

_____

_____

_____

The Tenth

Righteousness

"Doing wrong is like a joke to a fool, but wisdom is pleasure to a man of understanding."
~Proverbs 10:23 (ESV)

Proverbs 10 says much about the "righteous". Some translations use the word "godly" instead. Let's see what the word truly means, though.

The original Hebrew language uses righteous as a term for one who is just toward other men as well as in following God. Each of the words below are descriptors of righteousness:

- Right
- Correct
- Lawful

Righteousness is not a holy crown we put upon ourselves when we are in a relationship with God. Our actions toward our fellow man and toward God determine righteousness.

Are you pursuing God to know Him, to gain relationship with Him, to be taught by Him and then be imitators of His good ways?

The word "obedience" is associated with righteousness. It is found throughout Scripture, but it has unfortunately been given a negative connotation in today's lectern-thumping society of people loudly telling others what to do from a fear-based mindset.

What if obedience is born of love? A deep, heartfelt love for the One who created the world and breathed life into us. Perhaps obedience is also born of gratitude? A gratefulness for all that we have, for each new day, for the Father, Son and Spirit who have given us abundant, eternal life.

What if obedience leads us to freedom? For if we live within the simple guidelines God has given us, we are living from a place of alignment with Him, from a place of order and harmony. Freedom resides in that place of order and harmony, friends. Freedom will never reside in a place of chaos.

These thoughts are worth our consideration today.

"A new commandment I give to you, that you love one another: just as I have loved you, you also are to love one another."
~Jesus speaking in John 13:34 (ESV)

Proverbs Chapter 10
(ESV)

[1]The proverbs of Solomon. A wise son makes a glad father, but a foolish son is a sorrow to his mother.

[2]Treasures gained by wickedness do not profit, but righteousness delivers from death.

[3]The Lord does not let the righteous go hungry, but he thwarts the craving of the wicked.

[4]A slack hand causes poverty, but the hand of the diligent makes rich.

[5]He who gathers in summer is a prudent son, but he who sleeps in harvest is a son who brings shame.

[6]Blessings are on the head of the righteous, but the mouth of the wicked conceals violence.

[7]The memory of the righteous is a blessing, but the name of the wicked will rot.

[8]The wise of heart will receive commandments, but a babbling fool will come to ruin.

[9]Whoever walks in integrity walks securely, but he who makes his ways crooked will be found out.

[10]Whoever winks the eye causes trouble, and a babbling fool will come to ruin.

[11]The mouth of the righteous is a fountain of life, but the mouth of the wicked conceals violence.

[12]Hatred stirs up strife, but love covers all offenses.

[13]On the lips of him who has understanding, wisdom is found, but a rod is for the back of him who lacks sense.

[14]The wise lay up knowledge, but the mouth of a fool brings ruin near.

[15]A rich man's wealth is his strong city; the poverty of the poor is their ruin.

[16]The wage of the righteous leads to life, the gain of the wicked to sin.

[17]Whoever heeds instruction is on the path to life, but he who rejects reproof leads others astray.

[18]The one who conceals hatred has lying lips, and whoever utters slander is a fool.

[19]When words are many, transgression is not lacking, but whoever restrains his lips is prudent.

[20]The tongue of the righteous is choice silver, the heart of the wicked is of little worth.

[21]The lips of the righteous feed many, but fools die for lack of sense.

[22]The blessing of the Lord makes rich, and he adds no sorrow with it.

[23]Doing wrong is like a joke to a fool, but wisdom is pleasure to a man of understanding.

[24]What the wicked dreads will come upon him, but the desire of the righteous will be granted.

[25]When the tempest passes, the wicked is no more, but the righteous is established forever.

[26]Like vinegar to the teeth and smoke to the eyes, so is the sluggard to those who send him.

[27]The fear of the Lord prolongs life, but the years of the wicked will be short.

[28]The hope of the righteous brings joy, but the expectation of the wicked will perish.

[29]The way of the Lord is a stronghold to the blameless, but destruction to evildoers.

[30]The righteous will never be removed, but the wicked will not dwell in the land.

[31]The mouth of the righteous brings forth wisdom, but the perverse tongue will be cut off.

[32]The lips of the righteous know what is acceptable, but the mouth of the wicked, what is perverse.

Month One Journal Entry   Date: _____

_____

_____

_____

_____

_____

_____

_____

_____

_____

Month Two Journal Entry   Date: _____

_____

_____

_____

_____

_____

_____

_____

_____

_____

_____

Month Three Journal Entry   Date: _____

_____

_____

_____

_____

_____

_____

_____

_____

_____

Month Four Journal Entry   Date: _____

_____

_____

_____

_____

_____

_____

_____

_____

_____

Month Five Journal Entry   Date: _____

_____

_____

_____

_____

_____

_____

_____

_____

_____

_____

Month Six Journal Entry   Date: _____

_____

_____

_____

_____

_____

_____

_____

_____

_____

_____

Month Seven Journal Entry   Date: _____

_____

_____

_____

_____

_____

_____

_____

_____

_____

_____

Month Eight Journal Entry   Date: _____

_____

_____

_____

_____

_____

_____

_____

_____

_____

_____

_____

Month Nine Journal Entry   Date: _____

_____
_____
_____
_____
_____
_____
_____
_____
_____
_____

Month Ten Journal Entry   Date: _____

_____
_____
_____
_____
_____
_____
_____
_____
_____
_____

Month Eleven Journal Entry   Date: _____

_____

_____

_____

_____

_____

_____

_____

_____

_____

Month Twelve Journal Entry   Date: _____

_____

_____

_____

_____

_____

_____

_____

_____

_____

_____

The Eleventh

Integrity

"The integrity of the upright guides them, but the crookedness of the treacherous destroys them."
~Proverbs 11:3 (ESV)

Whether it's in the pursuit of wisdom, math, science, or even looking into the facts of the latest news or cultural condition, we must look beyond the superficial appearance of things to understand what they really mean.

Solomon often writes that we should gain understanding. This requires effort on our part: we must use the amazing minds God has given us – our intellect – to grasp it, and the power of our will to hold onto the understanding we've gained. It's so easy to waver back and forth once others tell us their opinions or situations influence us, but it's up to us to hold firmly onto the wisdom and understanding God first gave us. We're not to just absently listen to His words, or to graze lightly over them and then move on to the next pasture, but we should consider and process the concepts we're being shown. We must then be able to go a level deeper and see not only what that thing is but also what it is not to further enrich our understanding. The manner in which many of the Proverbs are written clearly shows that.

Let's use the word *integrity* from the verse above to better comprehend this. The word *integrity* is derived from the Hebrew word *tom*, which implies completeness. It is associated with today's English words *integrate* and *integer*. Think about what integrity is for a moment: something that is integrated is undivided or whole. When we read about integrity in Proverbs, that's important to think about – a person of integrity walks in wholeness. As much as we may want to believe we are people of integrity, we must take a realistic look within to see what we *are* as well as what we *are not*.

Are we truly whole?

Is there healing necessary in our lives that we are aware of, or that our close friends and family have told us we need to pursue?

Are we turning a deaf ear to or avoiding that healing?

We are not whole and cannot fully walk in the integrity we see ourselves in if we are avoiding a necessary healing. There will still be an incompleteness within, and we then fall short in the integrity department.

As you read today, look at the contrasts put together with each verse, and read with a fresh, intentional awareness. Solomon writes what the affirmative or desirable thing is in light of the negative condition or undesirable state. The desirable condition will be gained through understanding and will always lead us down wisdom's path.

Proverbs Chapter 11
(ESV)

¹A false balance is an abomination to the Lord, but a just weight is his delight.

²When pride comes, then comes disgrace, but with the humble is wisdom.

³The integrity of the upright guides them, but the crookedness of the treacherous destroys them.

⁴Riches do not profit in the day of wrath, but righteousness delivers from death.

⁵The righteousness of the blameless keeps his way straight, but the wicked falls by his own wickedness.

⁶The righteousness of the upright delivers them, but the treacherous are taken captive by their lust.

⁷When the wicked dies, his hope will perish, and the expectation of wealth perishes too.

⁸The righteous is delivered from trouble, and the wicked walks into it instead.

⁹With his mouth the godless man would destroy his neighbor, but by knowledge the righteous are delivered.

¹⁰When it goes well with the righteous, the city rejoices, and when the wicked perish there are shouts of gladness.

¹¹By the blessing of the upright a city is exalted, but by the mouth of the wicked it is overthrown.

¹²Whoever belittles his neighbor lacks sense, but a man of understanding remains silent.

¹³Whoever goes about slandering reveals secrets, but he who is trustworthy in spirit keeps a thing covered.

¹⁴Where there is no guidance, a people falls, but in an abundance of counselors there is safety.

¹⁵Whoever puts up security for a stranger will surely suffer harm, but he who hates striking hands in pledge is secure.

¹⁶A gracious woman gets honor, and violent men get riches.

¹⁷A man who is kind benefits himself, but a cruel man hurts himself.

¹⁸The wicked earns deceptive wages, but one who sows righteousness gets a sure reward.

¹⁹Whoever is steadfast in righteousness will live, but he who pursues evil will die.

²⁰Those of crooked heart are an abomination to the Lord, but those of blameless ways are his delight.

²¹Be assured, an evil person man will not go unpunished, but the offspring of the righteous will be delivered.

²²Like a gold ring in a pig's snout is a beautiful woman without discretion.

²³The desire of the righteous ends only in good, the expectation of the wicked in wrath.

²⁴One gives freely, yet grows all the richer, another withholds what he should give, and only suffers want.

²⁵Whoever brings blessing will be enriched, and one who waters will himself be watered.

²⁶The people curse him who holds back grain, but a blessing is on the head of him who sells it.

²⁷Whoever diligently seeks good seeks favor, but evil comes to him who searches for it.

²⁸Whoever trusts in his riches will fall, but the righteous will flourish like a green leaf.

²⁹Whoever troubles his own household will inherit the wind, and the fool will be servant to the wise of heart.

³⁰The fruit of the righteous is a tree of life, and whoever captures souls is wise.

³¹If the righteous is repaid on earth, how much more the wicked and the sinner!

Month One Journal Entry   Date: _____

_____

_____

_____

_____

_____

_____

_____

_____

Month Two Journal Entry   Date: _____

_____

_____

_____

_____

_____

_____

_____

_____

_____

Month Three Journal Entry   Date: _____

_____

_____

_____

_____

_____

_____

_____

_____

_____

_____

Month Four Journal Entry   Date: _____

_____

_____

_____

_____

_____

_____

_____

_____

_____

_____

Month Five Journal Entry   Date: _____

_____

_____

_____

_____

_____

_____

_____

_____

_____

_____

Month Six Journal Entry   Date: _____

_____

_____

_____

_____

_____

_____

_____

_____

_____

_____

Month Seven Journal Entry   Date: _____

_____

_____

_____

_____

_____

_____

_____

_____

_____

Month Eight Journal Entry   Date: _____

_____

_____

_____

_____

_____

_____

_____

_____

_____

Month Nine Journal Entry   Date: _____

_____

_____

_____

_____

_____

_____

_____

_____

_____

Month Ten Journal Entry   Date: _____

_____

_____

_____

_____

_____

_____

_____

_____

_____

Month Eleven Journal Entry   Date: _____

_____

_____

_____

_____

_____

_____

_____

_____

_____

Month Twelve Journal Entry   Date: _____

_____

_____

_____

_____

_____

_____

_____

_____

_____

The Twelfth

Disorder

"There is one who speaks rashly like the thrusts of a sword, but the tongue of the wise brings healing."
~Proverbs 12:18 (NASB)

Solomon continues the pattern we saw yesterday with intentional, repetitive contrasts between wise and unwise living. Let's continue reading to understand what each wise thing is and also what it is not.

Does it feel like some of this has already been said, maybe in a different way? Solomon is not repeating just to hear himself talk. Many of these proverbs were written as separate works, not necessarily in the order we encounter them in Scripture. The Book of Proverbs was assembled years after Solomon's death, as a collection of truths for good living. The way the book is put together does make it appear repetitive at times, but that is because Solomon saw fit to repeat certain important thoughts in different ways – examining them from many angles, so to speak. Repetition in Scripture is ultimately for emphasis, to enlighten the fullness of the thought. Repetition of a thing creates awareness, and Solomon knows that these important life principles cannot be overemphasized.

He speaks quite plainly in this chapter:

- *"...but he who hates reproof is stupid."* (There's just no way around that one.)
- *"...even the compassion of the wicked is cruel."*
- *"...the words of the wicked lie in wait for blood."*

He reminds us that those referred to here as the wicked or the evil ones have allowed the negativity they live by to penetrate to their very chaotic core – that same chaotic core we previously read about.

The disorderly, unbalanced core will never be corrected without repentance and a complete turning away from that chaos. Can you think of someone like this? It seems we've all crossed paths with such people and we've seen that as long as the chaotic core thrives it always draws more chaos in. Repentance and commitment to God's way open the door to order and open eyes to the healing that's needed.

Wisdom recognizes the chaotic people in our lives.

Wisdom tells us again and again to avoid them.

Wisdom gives us understanding that they do not spontaneously change. Chaos never changes to order on its own.

Solomon is also the author of Ecclesiastes. In it, he tells us there is nothing new under the sun. The people of our time are not unlike the people of his time. That's why the wisdom of his ancient words still echo truth today.

Proverbs Chapter 12
(NASB)

¹Whoever loves discipline loves knowledge, but he who hates reproof is stupid.

²A good man will obtain favor from the Lord, but He will condemn a man who devises evil.

³A man will not be established by wickedness, but the root of the righteous will not be moved.

⁴An excellent wife is the crown of her husband, but she who shames him is likes rottenness in his bones.

⁵The thoughts of the righteous are just, but the counsels of the wicked are deceitful.

⁶The words of the wicked lie in wait for blood, but the mouth of the upright will deliver them.

⁷The wicked are overthrown and are no more, but the house of the righteous will stand.

⁸A man will be praised according to his insight, but one of perverse mind will be despised.

⁹Better is he who is lightly esteemed and has a servant than he who honors himself and lacks bread.

¹⁰A righteous man has regard for the life of his animal, but even the compassion of the wicked is cruel.

¹¹He who tills his land will have plenty of bread, but he who pursues worthless things lacks sense.

¹²The wicked man desires the booty of evil men, but the root of the righteous yields fruit.

¹³An evil man is ensnared by the transgression of his lips, but the righteous will escape from trouble.

¹⁴A man will be satisfied with good by the fruit of his words, and the deeds of a man's hands will return to him.

¹⁵The way of a fool is right in his own eyes, but a wise man is he who listens to counsel.

¹⁶A fool's anger is known at once, but a prudent man conceals dishonor.

¹⁷He who speaks truth tells what is right, but a false witness, deceit.

¹⁸There is one who speaks rashly like the thrusts of a sword, but the tongue of the wise brings healing.

¹⁹Truthful lips will be established forever, but a lying tongue is only for a moment.

²⁰Deceit is in the heart of those who devise evil, but counselors of peace have joy.

²¹No harm befalls the righteous, but the wicked are filled with trouble.

²²Lying lips are an abomination to the Lord, but those who deal faithfully are His delight.

²³A prudent man conceals knowledge, but the heart of fools proclaims folly.

²⁴The hand of the diligent will rule, but the slack hand will be put to forced labor.

²⁵Anxiety in a man's heart weights it down, but a good word makes it glad.

²⁶The righteous is a guide to his neighbor, but the way of the wicked leads them astray.

²⁷A lazy man does not roast his prey, but the precious possession of a man is diligence.

²⁸In the way of righteousness is life, and in its pathway there is no death.

Month One Journal Entry   Date: _____

_____

_____

_____

_____

_____

_____

_____

_____

Month Two Journal Entry   Date: _____

_____

_____

_____

_____

_____

_____

_____

_____

Month Three Journal Entry   Date: _____

_____

_____

_____

_____

_____

_____

_____

_____

_____

Month Four Journal Entry   Date: _____

_____

_____

_____

_____

_____

_____

_____

_____

_____

_____

Month Five Journal Entry   Date: _____

_____

_____

_____

_____

_____

_____

_____

_____

_____

_____

Month Six Journal Entry   Date: _____

_____

_____

_____

_____

_____

_____

_____

_____

_____

_____

_____

Month Seven Journal Entry   Date: _____

_____

_____

_____

_____

_____

_____

_____

_____

_____

Month Eight Journal Entry   Date: _____

_____

_____

_____

_____

_____

_____

_____

_____

_____

Month Nine Journal Entry   Date: _____

_____
_____
_____
_____
_____
_____
_____
_____
_____
_____

Month Ten Journal Entry   Date: _____

_____
_____
_____
_____
_____
_____
_____
_____
_____
_____

Month Eleven Journal Entry   Date: _____

_____

_____

_____

_____

_____

_____

_____

_____

_____

_____

Month Twelve Journal Entry   Date: _____

_____

_____

_____

_____

_____

_____

_____

_____

_____

_____

The Thirteenth

The Process

*"Whoever walks with the wise becomes wise, but the companion of fools will
suffer harm."
~Proverbs 13:20 (ESV)*

I t's been nearly two weeks since this month's Proverbs journey began. You *are* growing in
wisdom if you are reading the words of Scripture with a purpose to understand.

Trust the process with God. He is faithful to perform what He says He will do. It is
happening.

The words of the Proverbs are not empty, but they are life to our souls and enlightenment
to our hearts and minds. As you continue to study, you'll find eye-opening moments happening in your daily life. You will have an awareness of a situation in a whole new way. You
may have been in that circumstance for months or years, but it will suddenly be as if you have
special eyeglasses on that magnify the truth in the midst of it all.

You'll see the disruptive core of the chaotic people that are speaking opinions to you or
telling you what to do, and you'll begin to realize they are not worthy of a voice in your life.
You may not be able to keep them from contact with you, but you'll recognize the choices
you have in *how* you allow them to associate with you.

You'll have thoughts of good dreams, good visions, things that will be for the good of
others as well as yourself, and you can begin to believe that God has put them there and is
speaking to you.

As you read today, friends, remember to thank God for His Scriptures that have endured
throughout century upon century of history.

Ask Him to speak to you and teach you through His Word.

Ask Him for wisdom, to give insight and understanding.

And ask Him that you would hear His voice today.

He is faithful to deliver the thing He has promised to those that please Him. Those that
would draw near to Him in spirit and truth please Him.

*"The Lord is close to all who call on him, yes, to all who call on him in truth."
~ Psalm 145:18 (NLT)*

*"For God is Spirit, so those who worship him must worship in spirit and in truth."
~ John 4:24 (NLT)*

Proverbs Chapter 13
(ESV)

¹A wise son hears his father's instruction, but a scoffer does not listen to rebuke.

²From the fruit of his mouth a man eats what is good, but the desire of the treacherous is for violence.

³Whoever guards his mouth preserves his life; he who opens wide his lips comes to ruin.

⁴The soul of the sluggard craves and gets nothing, while the soul of the diligent is richly supplied.

⁵The righteous hates falsehood, but the wicked brings shame and disgrace.

⁶Righteousness guards him whose way is blameless, but sin overthrows the wicked.

⁷One pretends to be rich, yet has nothing; another pretends to be poor, yet has great wealth.

⁸The ransom of a man's life is his wealth, but a poor man hears no threat.

⁹The light of the righteous rejoices, but the lamp of the wicked will be put out.

¹⁰By insolence come nothing but strife, but with those who take advice is wisdom.

¹¹Wealth gained hastily will dwindle, but whoever gathers little by little will increase it.

¹²Hope deferred makes the heart sick, but a desire fulfilled is a tree of life.

¹³Whoever despises the word brings destruction on himself, but he who reveres the command-ment will be rewarded.

¹⁴The teaching of the wise is a fountain of life, that one may turn away from the snares of death.

¹⁵Good sense wins favor, but the way of the treacherous is their ruin.

¹⁶Every prudent man acts with knowledge, but a fool flaunts his folly.

¹⁷A wicked messenger falls into trouble, but a faithful envoy brings healing.

¹⁸Poverty and disgrace come to him who ignores instruction, but whoever heeds reproof is honored.

¹⁹A desire fulfilled is sweet to the soul, but to turn away from evil is an abomination to fools.

²⁰Whoever walks with the wise becomes wise, but the companion of fools will suffer harm.

²¹Disaster pursues sinners, but the righteous are rewarded with good.

²²A good man leaves an inheritance to his children's children, but the sinner's wealth is laid up for the righteous.

²³The fallow ground of the poor would yield much food, but it is swept away through injustice.

²⁴Whoever spares the rod hates his son, but he who loves him is diligent to discipline him.

²⁵The righteous has enough to satisfy his appetite, but the belly of the wicked suffers want.

Month One Journal Entry   Date: _____

_____

_____

_____

_____

_____

_____

_____

_____

_____

_____

_____

Month Two Journal Entry   Date: _____

_____

_____

_____

_____

_____

_____

_____

_____

_____

_____

_____

Month Three Journal Entry   Date: _____

_____
_____
_____
_____
_____
_____
_____
_____
_____
_____

Month Four Journal Entry   Date: _____

_____
_____
_____
_____
_____
_____
_____
_____
_____
_____
_____

Month Five Journal Entry   Date: _____

_____

_____

_____

_____

_____

_____

_____

_____

Month Six Journal Entry   Date: _____

_____

_____

_____

_____

_____

_____

_____

_____

_____

_____

_____

Month Seven Journal Entry   Date: _____

_____

_____

_____

_____

_____

_____

_____

_____

_____

_____

Month Eight Journal Entry   Date: _____

_____

_____

_____

_____

_____

_____

_____

_____

_____

_____

Month Nine Journal Entry   Date: _____

_____

_____

_____

_____

_____

_____

_____

_____

_____

_____

Month Ten Journal Entry   Date: _____

_____

_____

_____

_____

_____

_____

_____

_____

_____

_____

Month Eleven Journal Entry   Date: _____

_____

_____

_____

_____

_____

_____

_____

_____

_____

_____

Month Twelve Journal Entry   Date: _____

_____

_____

_____

_____

_____

_____

_____

_____

_____

_____

The Fourteenth
Building

"The wise woman builds her house, but the foolish tears it down with her own hands."
~Proverbs 14:1 (NASB)

The house: a dwelling that often surrounds people in relationship. A shelter.

I have a friend I think of every month when I read this verse. She is a mentor to me and a maven in the art of keeping a home and living a well-loved life. My mind immediately pictures her as the wise woman Solomon speaks of.

Unfortunately, I've crossed paths with more people who have foolishly torn their spiritual houses, their relationships, their families, down with their own hands, mindsets, and words.

The ancient Hebrews of Solomon's realm built their own houses on family property. The land was an economic asset, but more importantly it was an inheritance to remain amongst the descendants of the original owner. The home on the land was their place of safety, truly standing as a physical testimony to the family's existence.

We read several references centered around the house and community in today's chapter.

People of the ancient times did not have housing developments, prefabricated homes or branded construction companies popping up home next to home next to home on postage stamp-sized lots. Families proudly built their homes with their own hands, or perhaps even bartered with or paid a craftsman for their assistance. They understood the effort it took to build a home and to create and maintain peaceful community relationships, because the property was designed to pass from generation to generation.

Who would work *against* the security their family needed, the shelter they had built, and intentionally tear it down?

Who would purposely bring wickedness and evil into their house?

What man would harm his neighbor, whose generations would continue to live adjacent to his own future generations, and leave a legacy of dissension?

So often, though, we do just that:

- We allow our tongue to control a situation harshly.
- We act without gratitude for what we have.
- We let impatience or bitterness get the best of us.
- We live with a spirit of competition, trying to prove ourselves better than those around us.
- We seek to control and manipulate those near us, often by applying undue pressure or the influence of fear.

We can be like human wrecking balls, tearing down our beautifully built spiritual homes piece by piece with unsavory thoughts, words and actions that do not serve or speak life to others.

Wisdom here desires to build us up that we would see the result of not walking wisely, so that in seeing what Wisdom is not, we would choose what she is and walk in truth and insight every day.

Proverbs Chapter 14
(NASB)

¹The wise woman builds her house, but the foolish tears it down with her own hands.

²He who walks in his uprightness fears the Lord, but he who is devious in his ways despises Him.

³In the mouth of the foolish is a rod for his back, but the lips of the wise will protect them.

⁴Where no oxen are, the manger is clean, but much revenue comes by the strength of the ox.

⁵A trustworthy witness will not lie, but a false witness utters lies.

⁶A scoffer seeks wisdom and finds none, but knowledge is easy to one who has understanding.

⁷Leave the presence of a fool, or you will not discern words of knowledge.

⁸The wisdom of the sensible is to understand his way, but the foolishness of fools is deceit.

⁹Fools mock at sin, but among the upright there is good will.

¹⁰The heart knows its own bitterness, and a stranger does not share its joy.

¹¹The house of the wicked will be destroyed, but the tent of the upright will flourish.

¹²There is a way which seems right to a man, but its end is the way of death.

¹³Even in laughter the heart may be in pain, and the end of joy may be grief.

¹⁴The backslider in heart will have his fill of his own ways, but a good man will be satisfied with his.

¹⁵The naïve believes everything, but the sensible man considers his steps.

¹⁶A wise man is cautious and turns away from evil, but a fool is arrogant and careless.

¹⁷A quick-tempered man acts foolishly, and a man of evil devices is hated.

¹⁸The naïve inherit foolishness, but the sensible are crowned with knowledge.

¹⁹The evil will bow down before the good, and the wicked at the gates of the righteous.

²⁰The poor is hated even by his neighbor, but those who love the rich are many.

[21]He who despises his neighbor sins, but happy is he who is gracious to the poor.

[22]Will they not go astray who devise evil? But kindness and truth will be to those who devise good.

[23]In all labor there is profit, but mere talk leads only to poverty.

[24]The crown of the wise is their riches, but the folly of fools is foolishness.

[25]A truthful witness saves lives, but he who utters lies is treacherous.

[26]In the fear of the Lord there is strong confidence, and his children will have refuge.

[27]The fear of the Lord is a fountain of life, that one may avoid the snares of death.

[28]In a multitude of people is a king's glory, but in the dearth of people is a prince's ruin.

[29]He who is slow to anger has great understanding, but he who is quick-tempered exalts folly.

[30]A tranquil heart is life to the body, but passion is rottenness to the bones.

[31]He who oppresses the poor taunts his Maker, but he who is gracious to the needy honors Him.

[32]The wicked is thrust down by his wrongdoing, but the righteous has a refuge when he dies.

[33]Wisdom rests in the heart of one who has understanding, but in the hearts of fools it is made known.

[34]Righteousness exalts a nation, but sin is a disgrace to any people.

[35]The king's favor is toward a servant who acts wisely, but his anger is toward him who acts shamefully.

Month One Journal Entry   Date: _____

_____
_____
_____
_____
_____
_____
_____
_____
_____
_____

Month Two Journal Entry   Date: _____

_____
_____
_____
_____
_____
_____
_____
_____
_____
_____
_____

Month Three Journal Entry   Date: _____

_____
_____
_____
_____
_____
_____
_____
_____
_____
_____

Month Four Journal Entry   Date: _____

_____
_____
_____
_____
_____
_____
_____
_____
_____
_____

Month Five Journal Entry   Date: _____

_____

_____

_____

_____

_____

_____

_____

_____

_____

Month Six Journal Entry   Date: _____

_____

_____

_____

_____

_____

_____

_____

_____

_____

Month Seven Journal Entry   Date: _____

_____

_____

_____

_____

_____

_____

_____

_____

_____

Month Eight Journal Entry   Date: _____

_____

_____

_____

_____

_____

_____

_____

_____

_____

_____

_____

Month Nine Journal Entry   Date: _____

_____
_____
_____
_____
_____
_____
_____
_____
_____
_____

Month Ten Journal Entry   Date: _____

_____
_____
_____
_____
_____
_____
_____
_____
_____
_____

Month Eleven Journal Entry   Date: _____

_____
_____
_____
_____
_____
_____
_____
_____
_____
_____

Month Twelve Journal Entry   Date: _____

_____
_____
_____
_____
_____
_____
_____
_____
_____
_____
_____

The Fifteenth
Words

"A wise person is hungry for knowledge while the fool feeds on trash."
~Proverbs 15:14 (NLT)

The world was spoken into existence.

Yes, God used words to create the universe, and we read about it as the Bible opens in Genesis, chapter 1.

If words were so important in the creative process to God, shouldn't they be important to us, too?

Our words should be the result of thought. Ideally, they are spoken in wisdom and never absent-mindedly or without care. We don't always see the truth of their creative power, but haven't we all felt our spirit shrink under the weight of negative, demeaning words spoken to us? What about the harsh words we've spoken to one of our children or even to a stranger in the heat of the moment? We've witnessed the crestfallen faces, the slumped shoulders and perhaps even anger in response to our assault.

Our words inspired that reaction.

Alternatively, we've also felt the joy bursting forth from loving, kind words that build us up inside. We have seen the smiles and light-heartedness our words can create for ourselves and others.

As you read today, look for all the references to the lips, words, the tongue, advice, saying, speaking, and anything else that has to do with words that are expressed. God never wastes His words, as I mentioned a few days back. He values the power they convey and never speaks without intention.

Sometimes it can seem challenging to find the right words, I know. It can be best to keep silent at times like that, despite our desire to be heard. The Proverbs say the same, in fact – repeatedly letting us know that it is better to keep silent than to speak rashly or like a fool.

Very wise words to live by, indeed.

"A glad heart makes a happy face; a broken heart crushes the spirit."
~Proverbs 15:13 (NLT)

Proverbs Chapter 15
(NLT)

[1]A gentle answer deflects anger, but harsh words make tempers flare.

[2]The tongue of the wise makes knowledge appealing, but the mouth of a fool belches out foolishness.

[3]The Lord is watching everywhere, keeping his eye on both the evil and the good.

[4]Gentle words are a tree of life; a deceitful tongue crushes the spirit.

[5]Only a fool despises a parent's discipline; whoever learns from correction is wise.

[6]There is treasure in the house of the godly, but the earnings of the wicked bring trouble.

[7]The lips of the wise give good advice; the heart of a fool has none to give.

[8]The Lord detests the sacrifice of the wicked, but he delights in the prayers of the upright.

[9]The Lord detests the way of the wicked, but he loves those who pursue godliness.

[10]Whoever abandons the right path will be severely disciplined; whoever hates correction will die.

[11]Even Death and Destruction hold no secrets from the Lord. How much more does he know the human heart!

[12]Mockers hate to be corrected, so they stay away from the wise.

[13]A glad heart makes a happy face; a broken heart crushes the spirit.

[14]A wise person is hungry for knowledge, while the fool feeds on trash.

[15]For the despondent, every day brings trouble; for the happy heart, life is a continual feast.

[16]Better to have little, with fear for the Lord, than to have great treasure and inner turmoil.

[17]A bowl of vegetables with someone you love is better than steak with someone you hate.

[18]A hot-tempered person starts fights; a cool-tempered person stops them.

[19]A lazy person's way is blocked with briers, but the path of the upright is an open highway.

²⁰Sensible children bring joy to their father; foolish children despise their mother.

²¹Foolishness brings joy to those with no sense; a sensible person stays on the right path.

²²Plans go wrong for lack of advice; many advisers bring success.

²³Everyone enjoys a fitting reply; it is wonderful to say the right thing at the right time!

²⁴The path of life leads upward for the wise; they leave the grave behind.

²⁵The Lord tears down the house of the proud, but he protects the property of widows.

²⁶The Lord detests evil plans, but he delights in pure words.

²⁷Greed brings grief to the whole family, but those who hate bribes will live.

²⁸The heart of the godly thinks carefully before speaking; the mouth of the wicked overflows with evil words.

²⁹The Lord is far from the wicked, but he hears the prayers of the righteous.

³⁰A cheerful look brings joy to the heart; good news makes for good health.

³¹If you listen to constructive criticism, you will be at home among the wise.

³²If you reject discipline, you only harm yourself; but if you listen to correction, you grow in understanding.

³³Fear of the Lord teaches wisdom; humility precedes honor.

Month One Journal Entry   Date: _____

_____

_____

_____

_____

_____

_____

_____

_____

_____

Month Two Journal Entry   Date: _____

_____

_____

_____

_____

_____

_____

_____

_____

_____

_____

Month Three Journal Entry   Date: _____

_____

_____

_____

_____

_____

_____

_____

_____

_____

Month Four Journal Entry   Date: _____

_____

_____

_____

_____

_____

_____

_____

_____

_____

Month Five Journal Entry   Date: _____

_____

_____

_____

_____

_____

_____

_____

_____

_____

_____

_____

Month Six Journal Entry   Date: _____

_____

_____

_____

_____

_____

_____

_____

_____

_____

_____

_____

Month Seven Journal Entry   Date: _____

_____
_____
_____
_____
_____
_____
_____
_____
_____
_____

Month Eight Journal Entry   Date: _____

_____
_____
_____
_____
_____
_____
_____
_____
_____
_____

Month Nine Journal Entry　　　Date: _____

_____

_____

_____

_____

_____

_____

_____

_____

_____

_____

Month Ten Journal Entry　　　Date: _____

_____

_____

_____

_____

_____

_____

_____

_____

_____

_____

_____

Month Eleven Journal Entry   Date: _____

_____

_____

_____

_____

_____

_____

_____

_____

_____

_____

_____

Month Twelve Journal Entry   Date: _____

_____

_____

_____

_____

_____

_____

_____

_____

_____

_____

_____

_____

The Sixteenth
Alignment

"The mind of man plans his way, but the Lord directs his steps."
~Proverbs 16:9 (NASB)

Oh, we can be fantastic planners, can't we? We see the result we want and plan every little detail to get us to that point. We have organizers, phone apps, timelines, colored pens and rulers that help us lay it all out right before our eyes. We work meticulously from the outside in.

And then life happens.

We are saddened as we see the fizzling out of the way that seemed so right from the external view, and we are left with mere fragments of the original plan. Sometimes we just cannot seem to regroup.

Proverbs reveals to us that, while the desires and ideas and thoughts may be in our mind, the plans are directed by God. He sees the entire beautiful tapestry of the world, and how each individual movement of the needle affects the entirety. He knows the best plan and doesn't need a vision board or app to assist Him.

He wants us to work from the inside out: from the prompting of the Holy Spirit inside of us – the Source of the vision–to the result. Living in orderly fashion.

So when we pray, friends, when we seek wisdom, understanding and guidance, know that it's okay not to know exactly how to do a thing. *Wisdom is not the how*. Let me say that again. Wisdom is *not* the how. Wisdom is the tool that equips us for understanding and the application of knowledge.

God has the how – *all* our how's – lined up.

What is required of us is alignment with Him.

He expects us to respond to the vision - the higher calling the Holy Spirit sparks in our hearts. *"Speak, Lord, for your servant is listening,"* are the words Eli the high priest gives to a very young Samuel in 1 Samuel 3:9 (NASB). The Lord had reached out to the boy three times, and as Eli realizes it is God Himself speaking to the child, he prepares Samuel to receive what the Lord would say.

Oh may we respond with the same willing spirit, understanding with childlike simplicity that the plans are God's and we just need to be the willing vessels that joyfully get to participate in their fulfillment. The plan will always be unveiled, step by step, in harmony with the glorious destiny He's calling each of us to.

Proverbs Chapter 16
(NASB)

¹The plans of the heart belong to man, but the answer of the tongue is from the Lord.

²All the ways of a man are clean in his own sight, but the Lord weighs the motives.

³Commit your works to the Lord and your plans will be established.

⁴The Lord has made everything for its own purpose, even the wicked for the day of evil.

⁵Everyone who is proud in heart is an abomination to the Lord; assuredly, he will not be unpunished.

⁶By lovingkindness and truth iniquity is atoned for, and by the fear of the Lord one keeps away from evil.

⁷When a man's ways are pleasing to the Lord, he makes even his enemies to be at peace with him.

⁸Better is a little with righteousness than great income with injustice.

⁹The mind of man plans his way, but the Lord directs his steps.

¹⁰A divine decision is in the lips of the king; his mouth should not err in judgment.

¹¹A just balance and scales belong to the Lord; all the weights of the bag are His concern.

¹²It is an abomination for kings to commit wicked acts, for a throne is established on righteousness.

¹³Righteous lips are the delight of kings, and he who speaks right is loved.

¹⁴The fury of a king is like messengers of death, but a wise man will appease it.

¹⁵In the light of a king's face is life, and his favor is like a cloud with the spring rain.

¹⁶How much better it is to get wisdom than gold! And to get understanding is to be chosen above silver.

¹⁷The highway of the upright is to depart from evil; he who watches his way preserves his life.

¹⁸Pride goes before destruction, and a haughty spirit before stumbling.

¹⁹It is better to be humble in spirit with the lowly than to divide the spoil with the proud.

²⁰He who gives attention to the word will find good, and blessed is he who trusts in the Lord.

²¹The wise in heart will be called understanding, and sweetness of speech increases persuasiveness.

²²Understanding is a fountain of life to one who has it, but the discipline of fools is folly.

²³The heart of the wise instructs his mouth and adds persuasiveness to his lips.

²⁴Pleasant words are a honeycomb, sweet to the soul and healing to the bones.

²⁵There is a way which seems right to a man, but its end is the way of death.

²⁶A worker's appetite works for him, for his hunger urges him on.

²⁷A worthless man digs up evil, while his words are like scorching fire.

²⁸A perverse man spreads strife, and a slanderer separates intimate friends.

²⁹A man of violence entices his neighbor and leads him in a way that is not good.

³⁰He who winks his eyes does so to devise perverse things; he who compresses his lips brings evil to pass.

³¹A gray head is a crown of glory; it is found in the way of righteousness.

³²He who is slow to anger is better than the mighty, and he who rules his spirit, than he who captures a city.

³³The lot is cast into the lap, but its every decision is from the Lord.

Month One Journal Entry   Date: _____

_____

_____

_____

_____

_____

_____

_____

_____

_____

Month Two Journal Entry   Date: _____

_____

_____

_____

_____

_____

_____

_____

_____

_____

_____

Month Three Journal Entry   Date: _____

_____

_____

_____

_____

_____

_____

_____

_____

_____

_____

Month Four Journal Entry   Date: _____

_____

_____

_____

_____

_____

_____

_____

_____

_____

_____

Month Five Journal Entry   Date: _____

_____

_____

_____

_____

_____

_____

_____

_____

_____

Month Six Journal Entry   Date: _____

_____

_____

_____

_____

_____

_____

_____

_____

_____

Month Seven Journal Entry   Date: _____

_____

_____

_____

_____

_____

_____

_____

_____

_____

Month Eight Journal Entry   Date: _____

_____

_____

_____

_____

_____

_____

_____

_____

_____

Month Nine Journal Entry   Date: _____

_____

_____

_____

_____

_____

_____

_____

_____

_____

Month Ten Journal Entry   Date: _____

_____

_____

_____

_____

_____

_____

_____

_____

_____

Month Eleven Journal Entry   Date: _____

_____

_____

_____

_____

_____

_____

_____

_____

_____

_____

Month Twelve Journal Entry   Date: _____

_____

_____

_____

_____

_____

_____

_____

_____

_____

_____

The Seventeenth

Intention

"He who restrains his words has knowledge, and he who has a cool spirit is a man of understanding."
~Proverbs 17:27 (NASB)

The Proverbs were originally written in Hebrew and, since they were penned by Solomon as he felt called to write them down throughout his life, it's easy to see how so many verses stand as independent thoughts. Chapters and verses were added to Scripture hundreds of years after Christ was born and were designed to assist as references to easily look up different passages of the Bible. Imagine trying to find what we now know as Proverbs 17:27 amongst the thousands of words contained in the book. Without designated chapters and verses it would be like searching for a needle in a haystack.

Just for a moment, try to picture a scribe or even the king himself, huddled over an expansive wooden desk lit by the rays of early morning sun, writing each wise saying upon a scroll of papyrus as the inspired words of the Holy Spirit were formed in Solomon's mind and spoken by his lips. There is such glorious peace, reverence and intimacy with God to behold in that image, and that beautiful, interactive relationship is ours, too, if we would just set the moments aside to spend with Him.

We are given opportunities for understanding through contrasting examples in this chapter, and this technique continues into Chapter 22. Solomon demonstrates through his word pictures that Wisdom can be achieved through practice and application, that Wisdom is available to all, and that Wisdom brings those who pursue her a life God considers fulfilling and righteous.

The message of mankind's intentional engagement in his own life - human responsibility for the one priceless life we are given and the impact we make - is seen throughout the book. Think about that today as you read. Are you living with a Kingdom focus that goes beyond just your immediate needs? Have you listened for the ideas God is giving you to grow and be fruitful, to use your unique gifts in fulfillment of your destiny? Perhaps you are sitting it out on the couch, letting the time for movement pass you by, judging yourself, thinking you're not ready?

Friends, trust that those ideas for good, ideas that align with God's love, His mercy, His righteous and just concern for all mankind – all those ideas you are resting on – are from God. Write them down. Find one of those ideas that you are able to walk in right now and take the first step, then let Him unveil the plan as you move forward.

This chapter contrasts foolish versus wise behavior, but the beautiful thing is that anyone can jump off the ship of fools to join the wise journey whenever they intentionally choose to change their course and advance their life in the best direction.

Proverbs Chapter 17
(NASB)

¹Better is a dry morsel and quietness with it than a house full of feasting with strife.

²A servant who acts wisely will rule over a son who acts shamefully, and will share in the inheritance among brothers.

³The refining pot is for silver and the furnace for gold, but the Lord tests hearts.

⁴An evildoer listens to wicked lips; a liar pays attention to a destructive tongue.

⁵He who mocks the poor taunts his Maker; he who rejoices at calamity will not go unpunished.

⁶Grandchildren are the crown of old men, and the glory of sons is their fathers.

⁷Excellent speech is not fitting for a fool, much less are lying lips to a prince.

⁸A bribe is a charm in the sight of its owner; wherever he turns, he prospers.

⁹He who conceals a transgression seeks love, but he who repeats a matter separates intimate friends.

¹⁰A rebuke goes deeper into one who has understanding than a hundred blows into a fool.

¹¹A rebellious man seeks only evil, so a cruel messenger will be sent against him.

¹²Let a man meet a bear robbed of her cubs, rather than a fool in his folly.

¹³He who returns evil for good, evil will not depart from his house.

¹⁴The beginning of strife is like letting out water, so abandon the quarrel before it breaks out.

¹⁵He who justifies the wicked and he who condemns the righteous, both of them alike are an abomination to the Lord.

¹⁶Why is there a price in the hand of a fool to buy wisdom, when he has no sense?

¹⁷A friend loves at all times, and a brother is born for adversity.

¹⁸A man lacking in sense pledges and becomes guarantor in the presence of his neighbor.

¹⁹He who loves transgression loves strife; he who raises his door seeks destruction.

²⁰He who has a crooked mind finds no good, and he who is perverted in his language falls into evil.

²¹He who sires a fool does so to his sorrow, and the father of a fool has no joy.

²²A joyful heart is good medicine, but a broken spirit dries up the bones.

²³A wicked man receives a bribe from the bosom to pervert the ways of justice.

²⁴Wisdom is in the presence of the one who has understanding, but the eyes of a fool are on the ends of the earth.

²⁵A foolish son is a grief to his father and bitterness to her who bore him.

²⁶It is also not good to fine the righteous, nor to strike the noble for their uprightness.

²⁷He who restrains his words has knowledge, and he who has a cool spirit is a man of understanding.

²⁸Even a fool, when he keeps silent, is considered wise; when he closes his lips, he is considered prudent.

Month One Journal Entry   Date: _____

_____
_____
_____
_____
_____
_____
_____
_____
_____
_____
_____

Month Two Journal Entry   Date: _____

_____
_____
_____
_____
_____
_____
_____
_____
_____
_____
_____

Month Three Journal Entry   Date: _____

_____

_____

_____

_____

_____

_____

_____

_____

_____

Month Four Journal Entry   Date: _____

_____

_____

_____

_____

_____

_____

_____

_____

_____

_____

Month Five Journal Entry   Date: _____

_____

_____

_____

_____

_____

_____

_____

_____

_____

Month Six Journal Entry   Date: _____

_____

_____

_____

_____

_____

_____

_____

_____

_____

Month Seven Journal Entry   Date: _____

_____

_____

_____

_____

_____

_____

_____

_____

_____

Month Eight Journal Entry   Date: _____

_____

_____

_____

_____

_____

_____

_____

_____

_____

_____

Month Nine Journal Entry   Date: _____

_____

_____

_____

_____

_____

_____

_____

_____

_____

_____

Month Ten Journal Entry   Date: _____

_____

_____

_____

_____

_____

_____

_____

_____

_____

_____

_____

Month Eleven Journal Entry   Date: _____

_____

_____

_____

_____

_____

_____

_____

_____

Month Twelve Journal Entry   Date: _____

_____

_____

_____

_____

_____

_____

_____

_____

The Eighteenth
Mission

"An intelligent heart acquires knowledge and the ear of the wise seeks knowledge."
~Proverbs 18:15 (ESV)

Have you noticed that the Book of Proverbs consistently sticks to the practical intent and opportunities for application mentioned in Chapter 1: that the wise would become wiser, that those with understanding would receive guidance? Unlike many other books of the Old Testament, Proverbs does not give historical accounts of the nation of Israel. It stays on its Wisdom mission, speaking principles of life.

How often do we know what our mission is but then get distracted, going down a wrong route or off on a tangent? Just one slight step off our mission personally inspired by God and we're chasing butterflies through fields we don't recognize. Next thing we know, the importance of the original mission no longer seems so critical, and it fades away as we take on the new self-directed mission to catch butterflies. Eventually we realize the butterfly catching was never truly the mission we were gifted to pursue, and we must find our way back to our mission's correct path.

Walking in our authentic calling, fulfilling our destiny, is the heart's cry of every man and woman. It creates a life of purpose, a well-loved life lived with enthusiasm as we pursue our mission. Don't be mistaken, *your* mission is one that only you are fully gifted to bring to fruition. There should be no fear of competition with others – God would not have us striving with others for our position. An inspired thought comes to mind and it resonates with our heart. It comes to us as good to serve others, a good we find ourselves passionate to fulfill. It comes to us, for us to act upon, because it is ours from God and we *shall* be equipped to act on it.

This is where our faith is called into action. We must act on the idea, we *must* be willing to step into it, and let God's plan unfold as we walk it out.

He never calls to do something that He will not equip us to do.

Wisdom tells us that.

"For I know the plans I have for you," says the Lord. "They are plans for good and not for disaster, to give you a future and a hope."
~ Jeremiah 29:11 (NLT)

Proverbs Chapter 18
(ESV)

¹Whoever isolates himself seeks his own desire; he breaks out against all sound judgment.

²A fool takes no pleasure in understanding, but only in expressing his opinion.

³When wickedness comes, contempt comes also, and with dishonor comes disgrace.

⁴The words of a man's mouth are deep waters; the fountain of wisdom is a bubbling brook.

⁵It is not good to be partial to the wicked or to deprive the righteous of justice.

⁶A fool's lips walk into a fight, and his mouth invites a beating.

⁷A fool's mouth is his ruin, and his lips are a snare to his soul.

⁸The words of a whisperer are like delicious morsels; they go down into the inner parts of the body.

⁹Whoever is slack in his work is a brother to him who destroys.

¹⁰The name of the Lord is a strong tower; the righteous man runs into it and is safe.

¹¹A rich man's wealth is his strong city, and like a high wall in his imagination.

¹²Before destruction a man's heart is haughty, but humility comes before honor.

¹³If one gives an answer before he hears, it is his folly and shame.

¹⁴A man's spirit will endure sickness, but a crushed spirit who can bear?

¹⁵An intelligent heart acquires knowledge, and the ear of the wise seeks knowledge.

¹⁶A man's gift makes room for him and brings him before the great.

¹⁷The one who states his case first seems right, until the other comes and examines him.

¹⁸The lot puts an end to quarrels and decides between powerful contenders.

¹⁹A brother offended is more unyielding than a strong city, and quarreling is like the bars of a castle.

[20]From the fruit of a man's mouth his stomach is satisfied; he is satisfied by the yield of his lips.

[21]Death and life are in the power of the tongue, and those who love it will eat its fruits.

[22]He who finds a wife finds a good thing and obtains favor from the Lord.

[23]The poor use entreaties, but the rich answer roughly.

[24]A man of many companions may come to ruin, but there is a friend who sticks closer than a brother.

Month One Journal Entry   Date: _____

_____

_____

_____

_____

_____

_____

_____

_____

_____

_____

_____

Month Two Journal Entry   Date: _____

_____

_____

_____

_____

_____

_____

_____

_____

_____

_____

_____

_____

Month Three Journal Entry   Date: _____

_____

_____

_____

_____

_____

_____

_____

_____

_____

Month Four Journal Entry   Date: _____

_____

_____

_____

_____

_____

_____

_____

_____

_____

_____

Month Five Journal Entry   Date: _____

_____
_____
_____
_____
_____
_____
_____
_____
_____
_____

Month Six Journal Entry   Date: _____

_____
_____
_____
_____
_____
_____
_____
_____
_____
_____

Month Seven Journal Entry   Date: _____

_____

_____

_____

_____

_____

_____

_____

_____

_____

_____

Month Eight Journal Entry   Date: _____

_____

_____

_____

_____

_____

_____

_____

_____

_____

_____

Month Nine Journal Entry   Date: _____

_____

_____

_____

_____

_____

_____

_____

_____

_____

Month Ten Journal Entry   Date: _____

_____

_____

_____

_____

_____

_____

_____

_____

_____

Month Eleven Journal Entry   Date: _____

_____

_____

_____

_____

_____

_____

_____

_____

_____

_____

Month Twelve Journal Entry   Date: _____

_____

_____

_____

_____

_____

_____

_____

_____

_____

_____

_____

The Nineteenth

Chaos

"Whoever gets sense loves his own soul; he who keeps understanding will discover good."
~Proverbs 19:8 (ESV)

We've seen now that Solomon repeatedly contrasts those that are wise, those that have insight and understanding, with the fool, the contentious, the one who seeks strife, with people of wrath and evil intent. These negative personality qualities, though they manifest in differing ways, come down to the same issue: they stem from chaos at the core.

Chaos = a lack of order = a state of confusion

A thing cannot be chaotic and orderly at the same time. It's just not possible for both conditions to dwell together. If chaos is the dominating characteristic, the entire thing is chaotic. This goes for people, too. We cannot be people of strife and have order as our natural state inside.

Order = peace = harmony = alignment with God

Humans cannot be fools, contentious, or people of evil intent and also have order as their natural state. Paul confirms this when he writes in 1 Corinthians 14:33 that God is not a God of confusion but that He is a God of peace and order. He is harmony through and through.

Understanding allows us to grasp this truth.

Wisdom tells us over and over again that chaos never becomes order on its own. This actually fulfills the natural law of entropy: everything progresses toward further disorder.

Chaotic people will continue to be chaotic, because they lack order in their inner man. Insight would have us know that every time we allow a chaotic person into our circle, we are opening a door for that influence of chaos to impact us.

Wisdom would tell us: (1) how to keep those situations from being part of our everyday experience and (2) what to do when we find ourselves there. Let's listen for her voice.

Proverbs Chapter 19
(ESV)

¹Better is a poor person who walks in his integrity than one who is crooked in speech and is a fool.

²Desire without knowledge is not good, and whoever makes haste with his feet misses his way.

³When a man's folly brings his way to ruin, his heart rages against the Lord.

⁴Wealth brings many new friends, but a poor man is deserted by his friend.

⁵A false witness will not go unpunished, and he who breathes out lies will not escape.

⁶Many seek the favor of a generous man, and everyone is a friend to a man who gives gifts.

⁷All a poor man's brothers hate him; how much more do his friends go far from him! He pursues them with words, but does not have them.

⁸Whoever gets sense loves his own soul; he who keeps understanding will discover good.

⁹A false witness will not go unpunished, and he who breathes out lies will perish.

¹⁰It is not fitting for a fool to live in luxury, much less for a slave to rule over princes.

¹¹Good sense makes one slow to anger, and it is his glory to overlook an offense.

¹²A king's wrath is like the growling of a lion, but his favor is like dew on the grass.

¹³A foolish son is ruin to his father, and a wife's quarreling is a continual dripping of rain.

¹⁴House and wealth are inherited from fathers, but a prudent wife is from the Lord.

¹⁵Slothfulness casts into a deep sleep, and an idle person will suffer hunger.

¹⁶Whoever keeps the commandment keeps his life; he who despises his ways will die.

¹⁷Whoever is generous to the poor lends to the Lord, and he will repay him for his deed.

¹⁸Discipline your son, for there is hope; do not set your heart on putting him to death.

¹⁹A man of great wrath will pay the penalty, for if you deliver him, you will only have to do it again.

²⁰Listen to advice and accept instruction, that you may gain wisdom in the future.

²¹Many are the plans in the mind of a man, but it is the purpose of the Lord that will stand.

²²What is desired in a man is steadfast love, and a poor man is better than a liar.

²³The fear of the Lord leads to life, and whoever has it rests satisfied; he will not be visited by harm.

²⁴The sluggard buries his hand in the dish and will not even bring it back to his mouth.

²⁵Strike a scoffer, and the simple will learn prudence; reprove a man of understanding, and he will gain knowledge.

²⁶He who does violence to his father and chases away his mother is a son who brings shame and reproach.

²⁷Cease to hear instruction, my son, and you will stray from the words of knowledge.

²⁸A worthless witness mocks at justice, and the mouth of the wicked devours iniquity.

²⁹Condemnation is ready for scoffers, and beating for the backs of fools.

Month One Journal Entry   Date: _____

_____

_____

_____

_____

_____

_____

_____

_____

_____

_____

Month Two Journal Entry   Date: _____

_____

_____

_____

_____

_____

_____

_____

_____

_____

_____

_____

Month Three Journal Entry   Date: _____

_____

_____

_____

_____

_____

_____

_____

_____

_____

Month Four Journal Entry   Date: _____

_____

_____

_____

_____

_____

_____

_____

_____

_____

Month Five Journal Entry   Date: _____

_____

_____

_____

_____

_____

_____

_____

_____

_____

_____

_____

Month Six Journal Entry   Date: _____

_____

_____

_____

_____

_____

_____

_____

_____

_____

_____

_____

_____

Month Seven Journal Entry   Date: _____

_____

_____

_____

_____

_____

_____

_____

_____

_____

_____

Month Eight Journal Entry   Date: _____

_____

_____

_____

_____

_____

_____

_____

_____

_____

Month Nine Journal Entry   Date: _____

_____

_____

_____

_____

_____

_____

_____

_____

_____

_____

Month Ten Journal Entry   Date: _____

_____

_____

_____

_____

_____

_____

_____

_____

_____

_____

Month Eleven Journal Entry   Date: _____

_____

_____

_____

_____

_____

_____

_____

_____

_____

_____

Month Twelve Journal Entry   Date: _____

_____

_____

_____

_____

_____

_____

_____

_____

_____

_____

_____

The Twentieth

Belief

"The spirit of a man is the lamp of the Lord, searching all the innermost parts of his being."
~Proverbs 20:27 (NASB)

*Y*esterday we talked about the law of entropy and how things naturally progress toward further disorder. Think of a fruit once it has been picked. It never progresses toward more growth, but advances through stages that ultimately cause rottenness if not eaten. Can you see why it's so important to have lives in alignment with God's will for us? Lives that align with His love, His equity, His righteousness, His heart for mankind. Aligning with Him will never lead us toward rottenness but will defy it.

This naturally leads to the thought: How does a chaotic person change?

We are not abandoned by God to disordered lives. He loves us and wants to see us living victoriously in freedom. Jesus came to perfectly demonstrate to a world in need the perfect qualities of the Father. The Amplified Classic Bible speaks of Jesus in *Hebrews 1:3, "He is the sole expression of the glory of God [the Light-being, the out-raying or radiance of the divine], and He is the perfect imprint and very image of [God's] nature, upholding and maintaining and guiding and propelling the universe by His mighty word of power. When He had by offering Himself accomplished our cleansing of sins and riddance of guilt, He sat down at the right hand of the divine Majesty on high…"*

When we believe in our hearts, in the very core of our being, that awesome reality of who Jesus is, we begin to recognize our shortcomings, we turn from them, and place ourselves on the path that defies the progress toward rottenness. The effort on our part, though, must be intentional. It is not just a quick prayer and momentary change of mind. It requires a studied change, planting and nurturing truth at the core, that comes as we study Scripture, learn from Jesus's teachings, and as we participate in understanding, gain insight, pursue healing and act with wisdom. It comes from daily denying ourselves those temporarily satisfying pleasures–even things as simple as a quick lashing out with the tongue at someone whom we believe deserves it - and pursuing God's authored way of order, patience and wisdom.

The changes come with consistent application. Consistency itself is defined by order. Sure, we may slip on our path, but we must choose to remain aligned with God. This all leads to true freedom, where the burdens of this world no longer hold us down.

What about others? When do we allow back in someone who has always been a chaotic presence in our lives? When do we believe they have changed? One sign will be good fruit shown in their lives.

"It is by his deeds that a lad distinguishes himself if his conduct is pure and right," says Proverbs 20:11 (NASB). Anyone can pay lip-service. Wisdom lets us see the truth. Know truth, know Wisdom, and trust the instincts they develop in you.

"Keeping away from strife is an honor for a man, but any fool will quarrel."
~ Proverbs 20:3 (NASB)

Proverbs Chapter 20
(NASB)

¹Wine is a mocker, strong drink a brawler, and whoever is intoxicated by it is not wise.

²The terror of a king is like the growling of a lion; he who provokes him to anger forfeits his own life.

³Keeping away from strife is an honor for a man, but any fool will quarrel.

⁴The sluggard does not plow after the autumn, so he begs during the harvest and has nothing.

⁵A plan in the heart of a man is like deep water, but a man of understanding draws it out.

⁶Many a man proclaims his own loyalty, but who can find a trustworthy man?

⁷A righteous man who walks in his integrity – how blessed are his sons after him.

⁸A king who sits on the throne of justice disperses all evil with his eyes.

⁹Who can say, "I have cleansed my heart, I am pure from my sin"?

¹⁰Differing weights and differing measures, both of them are abominable to the Lord.

¹¹It is by his deeds that a lad distinguishes himself if his conduct is pure and right.

¹²The hearing ear and the seeing eye, the Lord has made both of them.

¹³Do not love sleep, or you will become poor; open your eyes, and you will be satisfied with food.

¹⁴"Bad, bad," says the buyer, but when he goes his way, then he boasts.

¹⁵There is gold, and an abundance of jewels; but the lips of knowledge are a more precious thing.

¹⁶Take his garment when he becomes surety for a stranger; and for foreigners, hold him in pledge.

¹⁷Bread obtained by falsehood is sweet to a man, but afterward his mouth will be filled with gravel.

¹⁸Prepare plans by consultation, and make war by wise guidance.

¹⁹He who goes about as a slanderer reveals secrets, therefore do not associate with a gossip.

²⁰He wo curses his father or his mother, his lamp will go out in time of darkness.

²¹An inheritance gained hurriedly at the beginning will not be blessed in the end.

²²Do not say, "I will repay evil"; wait for the Lord, and He will save you.

²³Differing weights are an abomination to the Lord, and a false scale is not good.

²⁴Man's steps are ordained by the Lord, how then can man understand his way?

²⁵It is a trap for a man to say rashly, "It is holy!" and after the vows to make inquiry.

²⁶A wise king winnows the wicked, and drives the threshing wheel over them.

²⁷The spirit of man is the lamp of the Lord, searching all the innermost parts of his being.

²⁸Loyalty and truth preserve the king, and he upholds his throne by righteousness.

²⁹The glory of young men is their strength, and the honor of old men is their gray hair.

³⁰Stripes that wound scour away evil, and strokes reach the innermost parts.

Month One Journal Entry   Date: _____

_____

_____

_____

_____

_____

_____

_____

_____

_____

_____

_____

Month Two Journal Entry   Date: _____

_____

_____

_____

_____

_____

_____

_____

_____

_____

_____

_____

Month Three Journal Entry   Date: _____

_____

_____

_____

_____

_____

_____

_____

_____

_____

_____

_____

Month Four Journal Entry   Date: _____

_____

_____

_____

_____

_____

_____

_____

_____

_____

_____

_____

_____

Month Five Journal Entry   Date: _____

_____

_____

_____

_____

_____

_____

_____

_____

_____

_____

Month Six Journal Entry   Date: _____

_____

_____

_____

_____

_____

_____

_____

_____

_____

_____

Month Seven Journal Entry   Date: _____

_____

_____

_____

_____

_____

_____

_____

_____

_____

_____

Month Eight Journal Entry   Date: _____

_____

_____

_____

_____

_____

_____

_____

_____

_____

_____

_____

Month Nine Journal Entry   Date: _____

_____

_____

_____

_____

_____

_____

_____

_____

_____

Month Ten Journal Entry   Date: _____

_____

_____

_____

_____

_____

_____

_____

_____

_____

_____

Month Eleven Journal Entry   Date: _____

_____

_____

_____

_____

_____

_____

_____

_____

_____

Month Twelve Journal Entry   Date: _____

_____

_____

_____

_____

_____

_____

_____

_____

_____

The Twenty-First
Justice

"There is precious treasure and oil in the dwelling of the wise, but a foolish man swallows it up."
~Proverbs 21:20 (NASB)

Every proverb we read is true and leads us toward wisdom, but there are those "hidden treasure" verses that give us insight into the very heart of God.

One of those verses is in Chapter 21 and we may miss it if we aren't reading to intentionally gain insight. It echoes a message that's repeated throughout the Scriptures. Keep in mind, when God states something repeatedly, it's a call for us to sit up and really pay attention because what's being said is important to Him. Remember, He never wastes words.

"To do righteousness and justice is desired by the Lord more than sacrifice."
~Proverbs 21:3 (NASB)

We took a deeper look at what righteous originally meant back on the tenth. The ancient Hebrew language uses righteous as a term for one who is just toward other men as well as in following God.

What about justice? Justice is that which is reasonable and lawful. It is a judgment made from equity and a balanced perspective, not out of favor but out of right-ness.

We are repeatedly told to be righteous people throughout Scripture. Leaders are to administer justice without partiality or for gain. We are to be people who love with unselfish concern for others, a concern that seeks the best for them. We are not to manipulate or control others. We're told to look out for the orphan and widow, for they had no defenders to ensure they were treated righteously in ancient societies.

These expressions of equity are expressions of God's love that He would have us actively share toward those around us. We should become so aware of this standard of righteousness that it is second nature to us.

As we read Chapter 21 today, notice how verse 3 speaks of righteousness and justice but not as a random, standalone verse. It's tied to the verses before and after, telling a story. May we seek insight and understanding as we meditate on these words.

Proverbs Chapter 21
(NASB)

¹The king's heart is like channels of water in the hand of the Lord; He turns it wherever He wishes.

²Every man's way is right in his own eyes, but the Lord weighs the hearts.

³To do righteousness and justice is desired by the Lord more than sacrifice.

⁴Haughty eyes and a proud heart, the lamp of the wicked, is sin.

⁵The plans of the diligent lead surely to advantage, but everyone who is hasty comes surely to poverty.

⁶The acquisition of treasures by a lying tongue is a fleeting vapor, the pursuit of death.

⁷The violence of the wicked will drag them away, because they refuse to act with justice.

⁸The way of a guilty man is crooked, but as for the pure, his conduct is upright.

⁹It is better to live in a corner of a roof than in a house shared with a contentious woman.

¹⁰The soul of the wicked desires evil; his neighbor finds no favor in his eyes.

¹¹When the scoffer is punished, the naïve becomes wise; but when the wise is instructed, he receives knowledge.

¹²The righteous one considers the house of the wicked, turning the wicked to ruin.

¹³He who shuts his ear to the cry of the poor will also cry himself and not be answered.

¹⁴A gift in secret subdues anger, and a bribe in the bosom, strong wrath.

¹⁵The exercise of justice is joy for the righteous, but is terror to the workers of iniquity.

¹⁶A man who wanders from the way of understanding will rest in the assembly of the dead.

¹⁷He who loves pleasure will become a poor man; he who loves wine and oil will not become rich.

¹⁸The wicked is a ransom for the righteous, and the treacherous is in the place of the upright.

¹⁹It is better to live in a desert land than with a contentious and vexing woman.

²⁰There is precious treasure and oil in the dwelling of the wise, but a foolish man swallows it up.

²¹He who pursues righteousness and loyalty finds life, righteousness and honor.

²²A wise man scales the city of the mighty and brings down the stronghold in which they trust.

²³He who guards his mouth and his tongue, guards his soul from troubles.

²⁴"Proud," "Haughty," "Scoffer," are his names, who acts with insolent pride.

²⁵The desire of the sluggard puts him to death, for his hands refuse to work; ²⁶all day long he is craving, while the righteous gives and does not hold back.

²⁷The sacrifice of the wicked is an abomination, how much more when he brings it with evil intent!

²⁸A false witness will perish, but the man who listens to the truth will speak forever.

²⁹A wicked man displays a bold face, but as for the upright, he makes his way sure.

³⁰There is no wisdom and no understanding and no counsel against the Lord.

³¹The horse is prepared for the day of battle, but victory belongs to the Lord.

Month One Journal Entry   Date: _____

_____

_____

_____

_____

_____

_____

_____

_____

_____

_____

Month Two Journal Entry   Date: _____

_____

_____

_____

_____

_____

_____

_____

_____

_____

_____

Month Three Journal Entry   Date: _____

_____

_____

_____

_____

_____

_____

_____

_____

_____

Month Four Journal Entry   Date: _____

_____

_____

_____

_____

_____

_____

_____

_____

_____

Month Five Journal Entry   Date: _____

_____

_____

_____

_____

_____

_____

_____

_____

_____

_____

Month Six Journal Entry   Date: _____

_____

_____

_____

_____

_____

_____

_____

_____

_____

_____

_____

Month Seven Journal Entry   Date: _____

_____

_____

_____

_____

_____

_____

_____

_____

_____

Month Eight Journal Entry   Date: _____

_____

_____

_____

_____

_____

_____

_____

_____

_____

Month Nine Journal Entry   Date: _____

_____
_____
_____
_____
_____
_____
_____
_____
_____
_____
_____

Month Ten Journal Entry   Date: _____

_____
_____
_____
_____
_____
_____
_____
_____
_____
_____
_____
_____

Month Eleven Journal Entry   Date: _____

_____

_____

_____

_____

_____

_____

_____

_____

_____

Month Twelve Journal Entry   Date: _____

_____

_____

_____

_____

_____

_____

_____

_____

_____

The Twenty-Second
Love

"Incline your ear, and hear the words of the wise, and apply your heart to my knowledge, for it will be pleasant if you keep them within you, if all of them are ready on your lips."
~Proverbs 22:17-18 (ESV)

*Y*esterday we discussed the recurrent theme throughout Scripture that we be righteous and just people who do not offer "less than" treatment to the poor, widowed, orphaned, or even those *we* see as undeserving.

This theme is carried all the way into the New Testament as Jesus tells us in John 13:34-35 that He gives us a new commandment: *"...just as I have loved you, you also are to love one another. By this all people will know that you are my disciples, if you have love for one another." (ESV)*

"Love" as Jesus speaks it, as Jesus demonstrated it to all whose lives He lovingly touched, is the Greek word "agape" (pronounced ah-gah-PAY).

This word was rarely used in the Greek language before Jesus came on the scene, but He and His followers brought it to a more common understanding. It was not the erotic, emotional love that was seen in marriage, or the brotherly love of a friendship, but a love that uniquely reflects the heart of God. Agape is a love not based on emotions but expressed by doing things for the benefit of another, even if it comes at a cost to one's selfish desires. It is a love free of control over or manipulation of others.

It often comes as a new thing to the world around us when we act from that place of *agape*, even though Jesus spoke these words about 2,000 years ago. We live in a society that well understands erotic love and even brotherly love, a society where people naturally manipulate others to achieve their own desires, in a society where people don't think twice when they control others to get ahead.

Agape love calls the world to pay attention and grasp this incredible, strange action of God's kind of love. It's a thing the world often cannot comprehend, and ultimately reviles because it denies our selfish instincts that we are so comfortable putting in the forefront of our lives.

We finish up this month's reading through Proverbs in the next nine days, so hearken to the verses that speak of behavior toward the underserved - the poor, the afflicted, the widow, the orphan – and know that God's heart is for them. He seeks people with righteous hearts that will express His love toward them. He tells us that over and over again.

"For I desire steadfast love and not sacrifice, the knowledge of God rather than burnt offerings."
~Hosea 6:6 (ESV)

"Go and learn what this means: 'I desire mercy, and not sacrifice.'"
~Matthew 9:13 (ESV)

Proverbs Chapter 22
(ESV)

[1]A good name is to be chosen rather than great riches, and favor is better than silver or gold.

[2]The rich and the poor meet together; the Lord is the Maker of them all.

[3]The prudent sees danger and hides himself, but the simple go on and suffer for it.

[4]The reward for humility and fear of the Lord is riches and honor and life.

[5]Thorns and snares are in the way of the crooked; whoever guards his soul will keep far from them.

[6]Train up a child in the way he should go; even when he is old he will not depart from it.

[7]The rich rules over the poor, and the borrower is the slave of the lender.

[8]Whoever sows injustice will reap calamity, and the rod of his fury will fail.

[9]Whoever has a bountiful eye will be blessed, for he shares his bread with the poor.

[10]Drive out a scoffer, and strife will go out, and quarreling and abuse will cease.

[11]He who loves purity of heart, and whose speech is gracious, will have the king as his friend.

[12]The eyes of the Lord keep watch over knowledge, but he overthrows the words of the traitor.

[13]The sluggard says, "There is a lion outside! I shall be killed in the streets!"

[14]The mouth of forbidden women is a deep pit; he with whom the Lord is angry will fall into it.

[15]Folly is bound up in the heart of a child, but the rod of discipline drives it far from him.

[16]Whoever oppresses the poor to increase his own wealth, or gives to the rich, will only come to poverty.

[17]Incline your ear, and hear the words of the wise, and apply your heart to my knowledge, [18]for it will be pleasant if you keep them within you, if all of them are ready on your lips.

[19]That your trust may be in the Lord, I have made them known to you today, even to you.

²⁰Have I not written for you thirty sayings of counsel and knowledge, ²¹to make you know what is right and true, that you may give a true answer to those who sent you?

²²Do not rob the poor, because he is poor, or crush the afflicted at the gate, ²³for the Lord will plead their cause and rob of life those who rob them.

²⁴Make no friendship with a man given to anger, nor go with a wrathful man, ²⁵lest you learn his ways and entangle yourself in a snare.

²⁶Be not one of those who give pledges, who put up security for debts.

²⁷If you have nothing with which to pay, why should your bed be taken from under you?

²⁸Do not move the ancient landmark that your fathers have set.

²⁹Do you see a man skillful in his work?

He will stand before kings; he will not stand before obscure men.

Month One Journal Entry   Date: _____

_____
_____
_____
_____
_____
_____
_____
_____
_____
_____

Month Two Journal Entry   Date: _____

_____
_____
_____
_____
_____
_____
_____
_____
_____
_____

Month Three Journal Entry   Date: _____

_____

_____

_____

_____

_____

_____

_____

_____

_____

Month Four Journal Entry   Date: _____

_____

_____

_____

_____

_____

_____

_____

_____

_____

_____

Month Five Journal Entry   Date: _____

_____

_____

_____

_____

_____

_____

_____

_____

_____

_____

Month Six Journal Entry   Date: _____

_____

_____

_____

_____

_____

_____

_____

_____

_____

_____

Month Seven Journal Entry   Date: _____

_____

_____

_____

_____

_____

_____

_____

_____

_____

_____

Month Eight Journal Entry   Date: _____

_____

_____

_____

_____

_____

_____

_____

_____

_____

_____

Month Nine Journal Entry   Date: _____

_____
_____
_____
_____
_____
_____
_____
_____
_____
_____

Month Ten Journal Entry   Date: _____

_____
_____
_____
_____
_____
_____
_____
_____
_____
_____

Month Eleven Journal Entry   Date: _____

_____

_____

_____

_____

_____

_____

_____

_____

_____

_____

Month Twelve Journal Entry   Date: _____

_____

_____

_____

_____

_____

_____

_____

_____

_____

_____

_____

The Twenty-Third
Boundary Stones

"Buy the truth and do not sell it – wisdom, instruction and insight as well."
~Proverbs 23:23 (NIV)

Yesterday and today we read that no one should move the "ancient boundary stones". Some versions of Proverbs would say the "ancient landmarks." What does that have to do with wisdom?

Property ownership was a sign of security, provision, and wealth in the ancient Hebrew culture. When the Israelites moved into the land, each tribe was assigned a region to settle in, and each family was assigned a portion of land as their own.

The boundaries of one's property were established from the times of old, and so moving the stones that defined those boundaries was essentially cheating your neighbor of the land that was already theirs. It was lying by practice, denying someone else their God-ordained property.

It's not unlike when we set our own healthy boundaries in a relationship. They are there to help us feel secure and provided for. They let us and others know what we define as unacceptable behavior, at what point the line is crossed and their behavior will not be tolerated.

Establishing our boundaries empowers us as human beings - it is wealth to our inner man. When someone encroaches on our healthy boundaries, whether blatantly stepping over them, manipulating us to change "just for them," or even unknowingly pushing on them and expecting us to just go with the flow because that's how they see things should be, it is our responsibility to stand up for ourselves, call out the fact that they are trying to moving our boundary stones and defend those limits.

They are our boundary stones – you have your own and I have my own – and it is okay to say they are not to be moved. Yes, even to family members and friends. Yes, even to employers and customers. We are endowed with the freedom to establish and protect our own boundaries, to make them non-negotiable, and we can use the gift of graceful words spoken firmly to uphold them.

"Do not move an ancient boundary stone or encroach on the fields of the fatherless,
for their Defender is strong; he will take up their case against you."
~Proverbs 23:10 (NIV)

This particular verse speaks volumes to me, for I was born to a young mother who relinquished me for adoption. Until my adoption was finalized, I was an orphan and that is why the words of this verse speak to my heart so dearly. Though my birth father and birth mother released their care of me, my God and Defender never did. He has always stood for me, especially in the unseen moments. He gave me a home, a life story, a hope. He kept my boundary stones firmly placed when there was no one else to do it for me. He is truly the Good Father.

Proverbs Chapter 23
(NIV)

[1]When you sit to dine with a ruler, note well what is before you, [2]and put a knife to your throat if you are given to gluttony.

[3]Do not crave his delicacies, for that food is deceptive.

[4]Do not wear yourself out to get rich; do not trust your own cleverness.

[5]Cast but a glance at riches, and they are gone, for they will surely sprout wings and fly off to the sky like an eagle.

[6]Do not eat the food of a begrudging host, do not crave his delicacies; [7]for he is the kind of person who is always thinking about the cost.

"Eat and drink," he says to you, but his heart is not with you.

[8]You will vomit up the little you have eaten and will have wasted your compliments.

[9]Do not speak to fools, for they will scorn your prudent words.

[10]Do not move an ancient boundary stone or encroach on the fields of the fatherless, [11]for their Defender is strong; he will take up their case against you.

[12]Apply your heart to instruction and your ears to words of knowledge.

[13]Do not withhold discipline from a child; if you punish them with the rod, they will not die.

[14]Punish them with the rod and save them from death.

[15]My son, if your heart is wise, then my heart will be glad indeed; [16]my inmost being will rejoice when your lips speak what is right.

[17]Do not let your heart envy sinners, but always be zealous for the fear of the Lord.

[18]There is surely a future hope for you, and your hope will not be cut off.

[19]Listen, my son, and be wise, and set your heart on the right path: [20]do not join those who drink too much wine or gorge themselves on meat, [21]for drunkards and gluttons become poor, and drowsiness clothes them in rags.

[22]Listen to your father, who gave you life, and do not despise your mother when she is old.

²³Buy the truth and do not sell it – wisdom, instruction and insight as well.

²⁴The father of a righteous child has great joy; a man who fathers a wise son rejoices in him.

²⁵May your father and mother rejoice; may she who gave you birth be joyful!

²⁶My son, give me your heart and let your eyes delight in my ways, ²⁷for an adulterous woman is a deep pit, and a wayward wife is a narrow well.

²⁸Like a bandit she lies in wait and multiplies the unfaithful among men.

²⁹Who has woe? Who has sorrow? Who has strife? Who has complaints? Who has needless bruises? Who has bloodshot eyes?

³⁰Those who linger over wine, who go to sample bowls of mixed wine.

³¹Do not gaze at wine when it is red, when it sparkles in the cup, when it goes down smoothly!

³²In the end it bites like a snake and poisons like a viper.

³³Your eyes will see strange sights, and your mind will imagine confusing things.

³⁴You will be like one sleeping on the high seas, lying on top of the rigging.

³⁵"They hit me," you will say, "but I'm not hurt! They beat me, but I don't feel it! When will I wake up so I can find another drink?"

Month One Journal Entry   Date: _____

_____

_____

_____

_____

_____

_____

_____

_____

_____

Month Two Journal Entry   Date: _____

_____

_____

_____

_____

_____

_____

_____

_____

_____

Month Three Journal Entry   Date: _____

_____
_____
_____
_____
_____
_____
_____
_____
_____
_____

Month Four Journal Entry   Date: _____

_____
_____
_____
_____
_____
_____
_____
_____
_____
_____

Month Five Journal Entry   Date: _____

_____

_____

_____

_____

_____

_____

_____

_____

_____

_____

Month Six Journal Entry   Date: _____

_____

_____

_____

_____

_____

_____

_____

_____

_____

_____

_____

Month Seven Journal Entry   Date: _____

_____

_____

_____

_____

_____

_____

_____

_____

_____

Month Eight Journal Entry   Date: _____

_____

_____

_____

_____

_____

_____

_____

_____

_____

Month Nine Journal Entry   Date: _____

_____

_____

_____

_____

_____

_____

_____

_____

_____

_____

Month Ten Journal Entry   Date: _____

_____

_____

_____

_____

_____

_____

_____

_____

_____

_____

_____

Month Eleven Journal Entry   Date: _____

_____

_____

_____

_____

_____

_____

_____

_____

_____

Month Twelve Journal Entry   Date: _____

_____

_____

_____

_____

_____

_____

_____

_____

_____

The Twenty-Fourth
Unapologetic

"By wisdom a house is built, and by understanding it is established; by knowledge the rooms are filled with all precious and pleasant riches."
~Proverbs 24:3 (ESV)

Construction zones: we've all driven through, around, and near them. They aren't always for major projects like large-scale developments or road repairs. At times traffic is diverted for something more minor like maintenance on a home or even the simple installation of cable TV. Everything passing around the perimeter of the house has to change its behavior because of what's happening on the property, at least until the issues are dealt with.

Most property owners are unapologetic about it - it just is what it is, and they know all will be fine for everyone once the work is over. Those in traffic, though, have no idea of the who, what, why or when - they have to wait it out, perhaps even crawl it out, while the necessary work is accomplished.

Yet, when it comes to the most important works of all - the works of healing, course correcting, aligning ourselves with the God of order and His Holy Spirit – we often are neglectful, or we feel bad or even get downright apologetic for doing the necessary thing for ourselves.

Sometimes we feel bad about the effect on our families if we were to focus so much energy on ourselves and progress through the course correction, without considering the more important lasting positive impact that order and healing will have for years to come. We start to believe that remaining in dysfunction is preferable to pursuing healing, focusing on the immediate impact rather than the permanent core change.

Solomon talks to this head-on today in the verse above.

Just as a beautiful home comes from the talent of applying wisdom, knowledge and understanding to the design features, so our lives and relationships are filled with all precious and pleasant things by those methods too. Let's set our sights on acquiring wisdom, on acquiring knowledge, on acquiring understanding, and applying them each day. Let them decorate the rooms and hallways of our lives. Each of these characteristics take diligence in practice, for they are not automatically showered upon us once for all.

Understanding requires the choice to live in eyes-opened awareness that comes from truth (John 16:13 tells us the Spirit is truth). Living in truth means not only recognizing the condition of those around us but recognizing our own condition and need for personal growth or healing. We are not here just to see others' homes, though. We must care for our own and accept that it is okay to be in a construction zone as we build ourselves up, grow and heal.

God has repeatedly made it clear throughout the Book of Proverbs that wisdom, knowledge, understanding, and order are desirable for us and favored by Him; therefore, it is right that we devote the time, practice, and energy needed to fully align with Him and make these foundational in our lives.

Proverbs Chapter 24
(ESV)

¹Be not envious of evil men, nor desire to be with them, ²for their hearts devise violence, and their lips talk of trouble.

³By wisdom a house is built, and by understanding it is established; ⁴by knowledge the rooms are filled with all precious and pleasant riches.

⁵A wise man is full of strength, and a man of knowledge enhances his might, ⁶for by wise guidance you can wage your war, and in abundance of counselors there is victory.

⁷Wisdom is too high for a fool; in the gate he does not open his mouth.

⁸Whoever plans to do evil will be called a schemer.

⁹The devising of folly is sin, and the scoffer is an abomination to mankind.

¹⁰If you faint in the day of adversity, your strength is small.

¹¹Rescue those who are being taken away to death; hold back those who are stumbling to the slaughter.

¹²If you say, "Behold, we did not know this," does not he who weighs the heart perceive it?

Does not he who keeps watch over your soul know it, and will he not repay man according to his work?

¹³My son, eat honey, for it is good, and the drippings of the honeycomb are sweet to your taste.

¹⁴Know that wisdom is such to your soul; if you find it, there will be a future, and your hope will not be cut off.

¹⁵Lie not in wait as a wicked man against the dwelling of the righteous; do no violence to his home; ¹⁶for the righteous falls seven times and rises again, but the wicked stumble in times of calamity.

¹⁷Do not rejoice when your enemy falls, and let not your heart be glad when he stumbles, ¹⁸lest the Lord see it and be displeased, and turn away his anger from him.

¹⁹Fret not yourself because of evildoers, and be not envious of the wicked, ²⁰for the evil man has no future; the lamp of the wicked will be put out.

²¹My son, fear the Lord and the king, and do not join with those who do otherwise, ²²for disaster will arise suddenly from them, and who knows the ruin that will come from them both?

²³These also are sayings of the wise. Partiality in judging is not good.

²⁴Whoever says to the wicked, "You are in the right," will be cursed by peoples, abhorred by nations, ²⁵but those who rebuke the wicked will have delight, and a good blessing will come upon them.

²⁶Whoever gives an honest answer kisses the lips.

²⁷Prepare your work outside; get everything ready for yourself in the field, and after that build your house.

²⁸Be not a witness against your neighbor without cause, and do not deceive with your lips.

²⁹Do not say, "I will do to him as he has done to me; I will pay the man back for what he has done."

³⁰I passed by the field of a sluggard, by the vineyard of a man lacking sense, ³¹and behold, it was all overgrown with thorns; the ground was covered with nettles, and its stone wall was broken down.

³²Then I saw and considered it; I looked and received instruction.

³³A little sleep, a little slumber, a little folding of the hands to rest, ³⁴and poverty will come upon you like a robber, and want like an armed man.

Month One Journal Entry   Date: _____

_____

_____

_____

_____

_____

_____

_____

_____

_____

_____

Month Two Journal Entry   Date: _____

_____

_____

_____

_____

_____

_____

_____

_____

_____

_____

Month Three Journal Entry   Date: _____

_____

_____

_____

_____

_____

_____

_____

_____

_____

_____

_____

Month Four Journal Entry   Date: _____

_____

_____

_____

_____

_____

_____

_____

_____

_____

_____

_____

Month Five Journal Entry   Date: _____

_____

_____

_____

_____

_____

_____

_____

_____

_____

Month Six Journal Entry   Date: _____

_____

_____

_____

_____

_____

_____

_____

_____

_____

Month Seven Journal Entry   Date: _____

_____

_____

_____

_____

_____

_____

_____

_____

_____

Month Eight Journal Entry   Date: _____

_____

_____

_____

_____

_____

_____

_____

_____

_____

_____

_____

Month Nine Journal Entry   Date: _____

_____

_____

_____

_____

_____

_____

_____

_____

_____

_____

Month Ten Journal Entry   Date: _____

_____

_____

_____

_____

_____

_____

_____

_____

_____

_____

Month Eleven Journal Entry   Date: _____

_____

_____

_____

_____

_____

_____

_____

_____

_____

_____

_____

Month Twelve Journal Entry   Date: _____

_____

_____

_____

_____

_____

_____

_____

_____

_____

_____

_____

_____

The Twenty-Fifth
Legacy

"Whoever has no rule over his own spirit is like a city broken down, without walls."
~Proverbs 25:28 (NKJV)

Chapters 25-29 contain a second collection of Solomon's proverbs organized at the time of King Hezekiah, who reigned about 300 years after King Solomon. This proves that the complete Book of Proverbs did not take its lasting form until well after Solomon had passed on.

It is written of Hezekiah that he was a king who trusted in God, who removed public altars to false gods, who cleansed and restored the temple in Jerusalem, and re-instituted the Feast of Passover and the practice of the Jewish law, which had long been overlooked by Hezekiah's own father, King Ahaz, and others before him. It is possible that in the process of researching the ancient writings and cleaning out the temple, these other proverbs of Solomon were located and added to the previously known writings.

Hezekiah was moved with a heart that sought God, to restore his kingdom's unity to and honor the God who had established their nation - the One who had delivered them from oppression and slavery. He led a spiritual re-awakening in his land and prayed for his people.

We read of Hezekiah in 2 Kings 18:5-7, *"He trusted in the Lord God of Israel, so that after him was none like him among all the kings of Judah, nor any who were before him. For he held fast to the Lord; he did not depart from following Him, but kept His commandments, which the Lord had commanded Moses. The Lord was with him; he prospered wherever he went," (NKJV).* What beautiful words of legacy to have the Lord record forever in Scripture.

Have you ever thought about what God might leave as a record of your life? What would you hope He would convey to your generations of the life you lived? May we be faithful to leave memories of a life that held fast to Him, to His wisdom, His love, His righteousness; a life of joy in which the Lord was with us, prospering us as He did Hezekiah, wherever we go.

Proverbs Chapter 25
(NKJV)

¹These also are proverbs of Solomon which the men of Hezekiah king of Judah copied:

²It is the glory of God to conceal a matter, but the glory of kings is to search out a matter.

³As the heavens for height and the earth for depth, so the heart of kings is unsearchable.

⁴Take away the dross from silver, and it will go to the silversmith for jewelry, ⁵take away the wicked from before the king, and his throne will be established in righteousness.

⁶Do not exalt yourself in the presence of the king, and do not stand in the place of great men; ⁷for it is better that he say to you, "Come up here," than that you should be put lower in the presence of the prince, whom your eyes have seen.

⁸Do not go hastily to court; for what will you do in the end, when your neighbor has put you to shame?

⁹Debate your case with your neighbor himself, and do not disclose the secret to another; ¹⁰lest he who hears it expose your shame, and your reputation be ruined.

¹¹A word fitly spoken is like apples of gold in settings of silver.

¹²Like an earring of gold and an ornament of fine gold is a wise reprover to an obedient ear.

¹³Like the cold of snow in time of harvest is a faithful messenger to those who send him, for he refreshes the soul of his masters.

¹⁴Whoever falsely boasts of giving is like clouds and wind without rain.

¹⁵By long forbearance a ruler is persuaded, and a gentle tongue breaks a bone.

¹⁶Have you found honey? Eat only as much as you need, lest you be filled with it and vomit.

¹⁷Seldom set foot in your neighbor's house, lest he become weary of you and hate you.

¹⁸A man who bears false witness against his neighbor is like a club, a sword, and a sharp arrow.

¹⁹Confidence in an unfaithful man in time of trouble is like a bad tooth and a foot out of joint.

²⁰Like one who takes away a garment in cold weather, and like vinegar on soda, is one who sings songs to a heavy heart.

²¹If your enemy is hungry, give him bread to eat; and if he is thirsty, give him water to drink; ²²for so you will heap coals of fire on his head, and the Lord will reward you.

²³The north wind brings forth rain, and a backbiting tongue an angry countenance.

²⁴It is better to dwell in a corner of a housetop, than in a house shared with a contentious woman.

²⁵As cold water to a weary soul, so is good news from a far country.

²⁶A righteous man who falters before the wicked is like a murky spring and a polluted well.

²⁷It is not good to eat much honey; so to seek one's own glory is not glory.

²⁸Whoever has no rule over his own spirit is like a city broken down, without walls.

Month One Journal Entry   Date: _____

_____
_____
_____
_____
_____
_____
_____
_____
_____
_____

Month Two Journal Entry   Date: _____

_____
_____
_____
_____
_____
_____
_____
_____
_____
_____
_____
_____

Month Three Journal Entry   Date: _____

_____

_____

_____

_____

_____

_____

_____

_____

_____

Month Four Journal Entry   Date: _____

_____

_____

_____

_____

_____

_____

_____

_____

_____

_____

Month Five Journal Entry   Date: _____

_____

_____

_____

_____

_____

_____

_____

_____

_____

Month Six Journal Entry   Date: _____

_____

_____

_____

_____

_____

_____

_____

_____

_____

Month Seven Journal Entry   Date: _____

_____

_____

_____

_____

_____

_____

_____

_____

_____

Month Eight Journal Entry   Date: _____

_____

_____

_____

_____

_____

_____

_____

_____

_____

Month Nine Journal Entry   Date: _____

_____

_____

_____

_____

_____

_____

_____

_____

_____

_____

Month Ten Journal Entry   Date: _____

_____

_____

_____

_____

_____

_____

_____

_____

_____

_____

Month Eleven Journal Entry   Date: _____

_____

_____

_____

_____

_____

_____

_____

_____

_____

_____

_____

Month Twelve Journal Entry   Date: _____

_____

_____

_____

_____

_____

_____

_____

_____

_____

_____

_____

The Twenty-Sixth
The Sluggard

"As the door turns on its hinges, so does the sluggard on his bed."
~Proverbs 26:14 (NASB)

The sluggard is also described as lazy or the slothful in other translations. I can't help but wonder if sloths get a bad rap. They may move slowly but that is how they were designed by God. They still get life done, at the speed they were born to move at. Their momentum is not something they can change. Not so with people, though.

Proverbs does not mince words about those who are repeatedly reluctant to invest the energy required to help themselves. The wise words do not condemn or criticize for needing a time of rest and recovery; but they clearly speak to a habitually lazy lifestyle.

We see quite a few descriptive verses of the sluggard today:

- He shouts danger when there is none.
- He stretches his hand out to feed himself but it's too much effort to bring it back to his mouth.
- He is wiser in his own eyes than seven men of wisdom and discretion.

The warnings to the sluggard are sandwiched between words about the fool and the contentious man. They are all different expressions of the person with a chaotic heart. Let the context here speak to you.

Proverbs Chapter 26
(NASB)

¹Like snow in summer and like rain in harvest, so honor is not fitting for a fool.

²Like a sparrow in its flitting, like a swallow in its flying, so a curse without cause does not alight.

³A whip is for the horse, a bridle for the donkey, and a rod for the back of fools.

⁴Do not answer a fool according to his folly, or you will also be like him.

⁵Answer a fool as his folly deserves, that he not be wise in his own eyes.

⁶He cuts off his own feet and drinks violence who sends a message by the hand of a fool.

⁷Like the legs which are useless to the lame, so is a proverb in the mouth of fools.

⁸Like one who binds a stone in a sling, so is he who gives honor to a fool.

⁹Like a thorn which falls into the hand of a drunkard, so is a proverb in the mouth of fools.

¹⁰Like an archer who wounds everyone, so is he who hires a fool or who hires those who pass by.

¹¹Like a dog that returns to its vomit is a fool who repeats his folly.

¹²Do you see a man wise in his own eyes? There is more hope for a fool than for him.

¹³The sluggard says, "There is a lion in the road! A lion is in the open square!"

¹⁴As the door turns on its hinges, so does the sluggard on his bed.

¹⁵The sluggard buries his hand in the dish; he is weary of bringing it to his mouth again.

¹⁶The sluggard is wiser in his own eyes than seven men who can give a discreet answer.

¹⁷Like one who takes a dog by the ears is he who passes by and meddles with strife not belonging to him.

¹⁸Like a madman who throws firebrands, arrows, and death, ¹⁹so is the man who deceives his neighbor, and says, "Was I not joking?"

²⁰For lack of wood the fire goes out, and where there is no whisperer, contention quiets down.

²¹Like charcoal to hot embers and wood to fire, so is a contentious man to kindle strife.

²²The words of a whisperer are like dainty morsels, and they go down into the innermost parts of the body.

²³Like an earthen vessel overlaid with silver dross are burning lips and a wicked heart.

²⁴He who hates disguises it with his lips, but he lays up deceit in his heart.

²⁵When he speaks graciously, do not believe him, for there are seven abominations in his heart.

²⁶Though his hatred covers itself with guile, his wickedness will be revealed before the assembly.

²⁷He who digs a pit will fall into it, and he who rolls a stone, it will come back on him.

²⁸A lying tongue hates those it crushes, and a flattering mouth works ruin.

Month One Journal Entry   Date: _____

_____

_____

_____

_____

_____

_____

_____

_____

_____

_____

Month Two Journal Entry   Date: _____

_____

_____

_____

_____

_____

_____

_____

_____

_____

_____

Month Three Journal Entry   Date: _____

_____

_____

_____

_____

_____

_____

_____

_____

_____

Month Four Journal Entry   Date: _____

_____

_____

_____

_____

_____

_____

_____

_____

_____

_____

_____

Month Five Journal Entry   Date: _____

_____

_____

_____

_____

_____

_____

_____

_____

_____

_____

Month Six Journal Entry   Date: _____

_____

_____

_____

_____

_____

_____

_____

_____

_____

_____

Month Seven Journal Entry   Date: _____

_____

_____

_____

_____

_____

_____

_____

_____

_____

Month Eight Journal Entry   Date: _____

_____

_____

_____

_____

_____

_____

_____

_____

_____

Month Nine Journal Entry   Date: _____

_____

_____

_____

_____

_____

_____

_____

_____

_____

Month Ten Journal Entry   Date: _____

_____

_____

_____

_____

_____

_____

_____

_____

_____

Month Eleven Journal Entry   Date: _____

_____

_____

_____

_____

_____

_____

_____

_____

_____

Month Twelve Journal Entry   Date: _____

_____

_____

_____

_____

_____

_____

_____

_____

_____

_____

_____

_____

The Twenty-Seventh
Truth

"A prudent person foresees danger and takes precautions, the simpleton goes blindly
on and suffers the consequences."
~Proverbs 27:12 (NLT)

As we read today, let's focus on the essentials of any study in Scripture.

- Seek the One who opens our eyes to words of truth.
- Thank Him for these words that have endured generation upon generation, often at the peril of others' lives.
- Ask Him to speak to us through His word, to teach us by His word, to strengthen us - strengthen our inner man - with it.

We know that physical exercise profits the physical body, but are we exercising the spiritual man within?

Are we intentionally sitting amongst words of wisdom? Are we soaking them in, meditating on them, seeking understanding and insight? Are we dwelling in the presence of the Source who inspired those words? Have we invited Him along and asked Him to be with us? After all, who better to show us the truth than He who is Truth?

Jesus tells all of the apostles in John chapters 14 and 16 that when He left, His believers would have another Helper - the Spirit of Truth - and He would guide them into all truth. He tells them the Spirit currently dwells with them and would be in them once He left. He tells them the world cannot receive the Spirit because they neither see nor know Him.

We now know that those who believe have His Spirit living inside of them because they have invited Him in. If we are convinced and hold to be true that Jesus is the Son of God, that He lived and breathed and walked this earth to show us the characteristics of God lived out as a man (Hebrews 1:3) that we would be free from sin and death, and if we have expressed that belief, then the Holy Spirit – the Spirit of Truth - dwells within us. He is God, and He is capable of showing us all truth.

Hearken to His voice of truth speaking to you every day, in all things. Invite Him to fill and guide you each day, that your eyes, mind and heart would be open to receive, for He guides us ever to wisdom, clarity and truth. Trust that the ideas for good that come to you are from Him and walk in them.

Continually meditate on His word, that you would draw nearer to Him and hear Him ever more clearly.

Proverbs Chapter 27
(NLT)

¹Don't brag about tomorrow, since you don't know what the day will bring.

²Let someone else praise you, not your own mouth – a stranger, not your own lips.

³A stone is heavy and sand is weighty, but the resentment caused by a fool is even heavier.

⁴Anger is cruel, and wrath is like a flood, but jealousy is even more dangerous.

⁵An open rebuke is better than hidden love!

⁶Wounds from a sincere friend are better than many kisses from an enemy.

⁷A person who is full refuses honey, but even bitter food tastes sweet to the hungry.

⁸A person who strays from home is like a bird that strays from its nest.

⁹The heartfelt counsel of a friend is as sweet as perfume and incense.

¹⁰Never abandon a friend – either yours or your father's. When disaster strikes, you won't have to ask your brother for assistance. It's better to go to a neighbor than to a brother who lives far away.

¹¹Be wise, my child, and make my heart glad. Then I will be able to answer my critics.

¹²A prudent person foresees danger and takes precautions. The simpleton goes blindly on and suffers the consequences.

¹³Get security from someone who guarantees a stranger's debt. Get a deposit if he does it for foreigners.

¹⁴A loud and cheerful greeting early in the morning will be taken as a curse!

¹⁵A quarrelsome wife is as annoying as constant dripping on a rainy day.

¹⁶Stopping her complaints is like trying to stop the wind or trying to hold something with greased hands.

¹⁷As iron sharpens iron, so a friend sharpens a friend.

[18]As workers who tend a fig tree are allowed to eat the fruit, so workers who protect their employer's interests will be rewarded.

[19]As a face is reflected in water, so the heart reflects the real person.

[20]Just as Death and Destruction are never satisfied, so human desire is never satisfied.

[21]Fire tests the purity of silver and gold, but a person is tested by being praised.

[22]You cannot separate fools from their foolishness, even though you grind them like grain with mortar and pestle.

[23]Know the state of your flocks, and put your heart into caring for your herds, [24]for riches don't last forever, and the crown might not be passed to the next generation.

[25]After the hay is harvested and the new crop appears and the mountain grasses are gathered in, [26]your sheep will provide wool for clothing, and your goats will provide the price of a field.

[27]And you will have enough goats' milk for yourself, your family, and your servant girls.

Month One Journal Entry   Date: _____

_____

_____

_____

_____

_____

_____

_____

_____

_____

_____

_____

Month Two Journal Entry   Date: _____

_____

_____

_____

_____

_____

_____

_____

_____

_____

_____

_____

_____

Month Three Journal Entry   Date: _____

_____
_____
_____
_____
_____
_____
_____
_____
_____
_____
_____

Month Four Journal Entry   Date: _____

_____
_____
_____
_____
_____
_____
_____
_____
_____
_____
_____

Month Five Journal Entry   Date: _____

_____

_____

_____

_____

_____

_____

_____

_____

_____

_____

Month Six Journal Entry   Date: _____

_____

_____

_____

_____

_____

_____

_____

_____

_____

_____

_____

Month Seven Journal Entry   Date: _____

_____

_____

_____

_____

_____

_____

_____

_____

_____

_____

Month Eight Journal Entry   Date: _____

_____

_____

_____

_____

_____

_____

_____

_____

_____

_____

Month Nine Journal Entry   Date: _____

_____

_____

_____

_____

_____

_____

_____

_____

_____

_____

Month Ten Journal Entry   Date: _____

_____

_____

_____

_____

_____

_____

_____

_____

_____

_____

_____

Month Eleven Journal Entry   Date: _____

_____

_____

_____

_____

_____

_____

_____

_____

_____

_____

Month Twelve Journal Entry   Date: _____

_____

_____

_____

_____

_____

_____

_____

_____

_____

_____

_____

The Twenty-Eighth
The Heart

"He who trusts in his own heart is a fool, but he who walks wisely will be delivered."
~Proverbs 28:26 (NASB)

Often referred to in daily conversation as the container for so many emotions, the heart plays a vital role in our physical health. We read in Scripture, though, when it comes to emotional awareness, that our hearts can deceive us. Yet people often say that we should follow our hearts' leading.

Where does the answer lie?

It lies in knowing ourselves.

It is true that emotions are known to be stored in organs like the heart. Ancient medicine says the heart is the place where happiness and sadness are stored, hence words like "broken-hearted" used to describe profound sadness, or telling someone, "You've made my heart happy," when they've pleased you.

When we have gained true insight into our own inner person, when we've looked inside with the intensity with which we often look at others, we will see *why* we do what we do, and what foundations our decisions are built upon.

Are we making decisions based on patterned responses or paradigms we've acquired throughout our lives? Are we choosing things because we feel bad telling someone the truth, or because we feel bad about how our actions may be interpreted? Perhaps we are embarrassed by something and making a choice based on that? We may think that we are righteously letting our hearts lead us, but leading with an emotion that's tainted with pride, fear, or is pattern-driven, means we are using a preset bias to perhaps make a critical decision that needs to be evaluated in light of truth. Bias is not the place to decide from.

We have the responsibility to ourselves and those around us to correct decision-making built on emotional and faulty pretenses once we've developed an awareness of where our decisions are coming from. It's our job to delete faulty programming and reset ourselves to proper functioning condition. This is another opportunity to allow necessary healing into our lives.

Our decisions should not be based purely on emotional bias or sway, but should be founded on the guidance of Wisdom, knowledge, truth and understanding. This Book of Proverbs give us the guidance Wisdom speaks, enabling us to use truth to choose beyond our heart's emotions, that we would find ourselves on the right path of decision.

Turn to Chapter 32, "Living in Practice," after journaling today if you are reading this entry on the final day of February.

Proverbs Chapter 28
(NASB)

¹The wicked flee when no one is pursuing, but the righteous are bold as a lion.

²By the transgression of a land many are its princes, but by a man of understanding and knowledge, so it endures.

³A poor man who oppresses the lowly is like a driving rain which leaves no food.

⁴Those who forsake the law praise the wicked, but those who keep the law strive with them.

⁵Evil men do not understand justice, but those who seek the Lord understand all things.

⁶Better is the poor who walks in his integrity than he who is crooked though he be rich.

⁷He who keeps the law is a discerning son, but he who is a companion of gluttons humiliates his father.

⁸He who increases his wealth by interest and usury gathers it for him who is gracious to the poor.

⁹He who turns away his ear from listening to the law, even his prayer is an abomination.

¹⁰He who leads the upright astray in an evil way will himself fall into his own pit, but the blameless will inherit good.

¹¹The rich man is wise in his own eyes, but the poor who has understanding sees through him.

¹²When the righteous triumph, there is great glory, but when the wicked rise, men hide themselves.

¹³He who conceals his transgressions will not prosper, but he who confesses and forsakes them will find compassion.

¹⁴How blessed is the man who fears always, but he who hardens his heart will fall into calamity.

¹⁵Like a roaring lion and a rushing bear is a wicked ruler over a poor people.

¹⁶A leader who is a great oppressor lacks understanding, but he who hates unjust gain will prolong his days.

¹⁷A man who is laden with the guilt of human blood will be a fugitive until death; let no one support him.

[18]He who walks blamelessly will be delivered, but he who is crooked will fall all at once.

[19]He who tills his land will have plenty of food, but he who follows empty pursuits will have poverty in plenty.

[20]A faithful man will abound with blessings, but he who makes haste to be rich will not go unpunished.

[21]To show partiality is not good, because for a piece of bread a man will transgress.

[22]A man with an evil eye hastens after wealth and does not know that want will come upon him.

[23]He who rebukes a man will afterward find more favor than he who flatters with the tongue.

[24]He who robs his father or his mother and says, "It is not a transgression," is the companion of a man who destroys.

[25]An arrogant man stirs up strife, but he who trusts in the Lord will prosper.

[26]He who trusts in his own heart is a fool, but he who walks wisely will be delivered.

[27]He who gives to the poor will never want, but he who shuts his eyes will have many curses.

[28]When the wicked rise, men hide themselves; but when they perish, the righteous increase.

Month One Journal Entry   Date: _____

_____

_____

_____

_____

_____

_____

_____

_____

_____

_____

Month Two Journal Entry   Date: _____

_____

_____

_____

_____

_____

_____

_____

_____

_____

_____

Month Three Journal Entry   Date: _____

_____

_____

_____

_____

_____

_____

_____

_____

_____

Month Four Journal Entry   Date: _____

_____

_____

_____

_____

_____

_____

_____

_____

_____

Month Five Journal Entry   Date: _____

_____

_____

_____

_____

_____

_____

_____

_____

_____

Month Six Journal Entry   Date: _____

_____

_____

_____

_____

_____

_____

_____

_____

_____

_____

Month Seven Journal Entry   Date: _____

_____

_____

_____

_____

_____

_____

_____

_____

_____

_____

Month Eight Journal Entry   Date: _____

_____

_____

_____

_____

_____

_____

_____

_____

_____

_____

_____

Month Nine Journal Entry   Date: _____

_____

_____

_____

_____

_____

_____

_____

_____

_____

_____

Month Ten Journal Entry   Date: _____

_____

_____

_____

_____

_____

_____

_____

_____

_____

_____

Month Eleven Journal Entry   Date: _____

_____

_____

_____

_____

_____

_____

_____

_____

_____

_____

_____

Month Twelve Journal Entry   Date: _____

_____

_____

_____

_____

_____

_____

_____

_____

_____

_____

_____

The Twenty-Ninth
Contrast

"The righteous is concerned for the rights of the poor, the wicked does not under-
stand such concern."
~Proverbs 29:7 (NASB)

*C*hapter 29 of Proverbs is the final chapter confidently attributed to King Solomon's writings. Chapters 27 through 29 have been sets of warning and instruction, often using the concept of contrasting and comparing between just and wise behavior and unwise behavior.

The unwise person is often described from the same set of words: contentious, rebellious, foolish, crooked, wicked, full of strife, scoffer, mocker, sluggard. As we discussed earlier in the month, the core behavior in all of these comes from internal chaos.

Chaos will never naturally become order, but we can change our own chaotic lifestyle with an active repentant choice accompanied by mindful effort and intention. We don't just say we're sorry to God and the people we've hurt and then walk away, mindlessly. Our role in repentance is to change our behavior or turn it around. This means that effort is required on our part – we must be intentional, we must learn and grow, we must be engaged participants and not just bystanders in our own lives. As we daily walk in the knowledge and power of the Holy Spirit and repeatedly *practice* wise behavior, we will change those old ways to new ways in righteousness, justice, equity and love.

Reading wisdom literature like Proverbs daily, monthly, year after year, enables us to form a practice focused on gaining insight, understanding, and the application of knowledge. It's a solid way to build ourselves up on a foundation of truth and wisdom that will not fail.

Turn to Chapter 32, "Living in Practice," after journaling today if you are reading this entry on the final day of February.

Proverbs Chapter 29
(NASB)

[1]A man who hardens his neck after much reproof will suddenly be broken beyond remedy.

[2]When the righteous increase, the people rejoice, but when a wicked man rules, people groan.

[3]A man who loves wisdom makes his father glad, but he who keeps company with harlots wastes his wealth.

[4]The king gives stability to the land by justice, but a man who takes bribes overthrows it.

[5]A man who flatters his neighbor is spreading a net for his steps.

[6]By transgression an evil man is ensnared, but the righteous sings and rejoices.

[7]The righteous is concerned for the rights of the poor, the wicked does not understand such concern.

[8]Scorners set a city aflame, but wise men turn away anger.

[9]When a wise man has a controversy with a foolish man, the foolish man either rages or laughs, and there is no rest.

[10]Men of bloodshed hate the blameless, but the upright are concerned for his life.

[11]A fool always loses his temper, but a wise man holds it back.

[12]If a ruler pays attention to falsehood, all his ministers become wicked.

[13]The poor man and the oppressor have this in common: the Lord gives light to the eyes of both.

[14]If a king judges the poor with truth, his throne will be established forever.

[15]The rod and reproof give wisdom, but a child who gets his own way brings shame to his mother.

[16]When the wicked increase, transgression increases; but the righteous will see their fall.

[17]Correct your son, and he will give you comfort; he will also delight your soul.

[18]Where there is no vision, the people are unrestrained, but happy is he who keeps the law.

¹⁹A slave will not be instructed by words alone; for though he understands, there will be no response.

²⁰Do you see a man who is hasty in his words? There is more hope for a fool than for him.

²¹He who pampers his slave from childhood will in the end find him to be a son.

²²An angry man stirs up strife, and a hot-tempered man abounds in transgression.

²³A man's pride will bring him low, but a humble spirit will obtain honor.

²⁴He who is a partner with a thief hates his own life; he hears the oath but tells nothing.

²⁵The fear of man brings a snare, but he who trusts in the Lord will be exalted.

²⁶Many seek the ruler's favor, but justice for man comes from the Lord.

²⁷An unjust man is abominable to the righteous, and he who is upright in the way is abominable to the wicked.

Month One Journal Entry   Date: _____

_____
_____
_____
_____
_____
_____
_____

_____
_____
_____
_____

Month Two Journal Entry   Date: _____

_____
_____
_____
_____
_____
_____
_____
_____
_____
_____
_____
_____

Month Three Journal Entry   Date: _____

_____

_____

_____

_____

_____

_____

_____

_____

_____

_____

Month Four Journal Entry   Date: _____

_____

_____

_____

_____

_____

_____

_____

_____

_____

_____

Month Five Journal Entry   Date: _____

_____

_____

_____

_____

_____

_____

_____

_____

_____

Month Six Journal Entry   Date: _____

_____

_____

_____

_____

_____

_____

_____

_____

_____

Month Seven Journal Entry   Date: _____

_____

_____

_____

_____

_____

_____

_____

_____

_____

_____

Month Eight Journal Entry   Date: _____

_____

_____

_____

_____

_____

_____

_____

_____

_____

_____

Month Nine Journal Entry   Date: _____

_____

_____

_____

_____

_____

_____

_____

_____

_____

_____

Month Ten Journal Entry   Date: _____

_____

_____

_____

_____

_____

_____

_____

_____

_____

_____

Month Eleven Journal Entry   Date: _____

_____

_____

_____

_____

_____

_____

_____

_____

_____

Month Twelve Journal Entry   Date: _____

_____

_____

_____

_____

_____

_____

_____

_____

_____

The Thirtieth

Digging Deeper

"Every word of God is flawless; he is a shield to those who take refuge in him."
~Proverbs 30:5 (NIV)

Today we'll read not Solomon's sayings, but the sayings of Agur son of Jakeh.
History doesn't paint much of a picture of him for us. Agur tells us in verse 1 that he is the son of Jakeh, and while that was obviously a key part of his identity that distinguished him from all other Agurs, that's pretty much all we know about him. Neither of these men are mentioned again in Scripture.

Strong's Exhaustive Concordance of the Bible tells us Agur means "gathered." Some hypothesize that Agur, rather than a name, is more of a description of the man who put this particular chapter together - that he was a "gatherer" of the sayings of others.

Whoever he was, this chapter is fully attributed to Agur as an "inspired utterance" or "oracle," as it is called in other translations.

I encourage you to always do your own research with credible sources like *Strong's Concordance* to dig deeper when you encounter a word, phrase or name that you feel needs greater insight. It's always good to begin your time reading Scripture asking God to reveal His word to you. Trust that He will do so and read the passages to gain understanding. Do your best to understand within the context of what is written, and then look up the words, the terms, the maps or history when you come to something that's not quite clear, using the understanding and wisdom He's given you to determine what is valid and what's not. Don't just accept what someone else says a thing means, but look for the foundational principles and references that give that thing its meaning.

Strong's Exhaustive Concordance of the Bible is a comprehensive work that was first published by James Strong in 1890. It is a reference for the King James Bible, which indexes the original Hebrew, Chaldee (the language of the Babylonians), and Greek words and meanings for every word in that text. It's an incredibly valuable asset to anyone searching for the rich meaning of the original language when studying the Bible. Other great tools include lexicons, Bible dictionaries and maps of the ancient Middle Eastern world.

Turn to Chapter 32, "Living in Practice," after journaling today if you are reading this entry on the 30th of April, June, September or November.

Proverbs Chapter 30
(NIV)

¹The sayings of Agur son of Jakeh – an inspired utterance. This man's utterance to Ithiel: "I am weary, God, but I can prevail.

²Surely I am only a brute, not a man; I do not have human understanding.

³I have not learned wisdom, nor have I attained to the knowledge of the Holy One.

⁴Who has gone up to heaven and come down? Whose hands have gathered up the wind? Who has wrapped up the waters in a cloak? Who has established all the ends of the earth? What is his name, and what is the name of his son? Surely you know!

⁵"Every word of God is flawless; he is a shield to those who take refuge in him.

⁶Do not add to his words, or he will rebuke you and prove you a liar.

⁷"Two things I ask of you, Lord; do not refuse me before I die: ⁸Keep falsehood and lies far from me; give me neither poverty nor riches, but give me only my daily bread.

⁹Otherwise, I may have too much and disown you and say, 'Who is the Lord?' Or I may become poor and steal, and so dishonor the name of my God.

¹⁰"Do not slander a servant to their master, or they will curse you, and you will pay for it.

¹¹"There are those who curse their fathers and do not bless their mothers; ¹²those who are pure in their own eyes and yet are not cleansed of their filth; ¹³those whose eyes are ever so haughty, whose glances are so disdainful; ¹⁴those whose teeth are swords and whose jaws are set with knives to devour the poor from the earth and the needy from among mankind.

¹⁵"The leech has two daughters. 'Give! Give!' they cry. "There are three things that are never satisfied, four that never say, 'Enough!': ¹⁶the grave, the barren womb, land, which is never satisfied with water, and fire, which never says, 'Enough!"

¹⁷"The eye that mocks a father, that scorns an aged mother, will be pecked out by the ravens of the valley, will be eaten by the vultures.

¹⁸"There are three things that are too amazing for me, four that I do not understand: ¹⁹the way of an eagle in the sky, the way of a snake on a rock, the way of a ship on the high seas, and the way of a man with a young woman.

[20]"This is the way of an adulterous woman: She eats and wipes her mouth and says, 'I've done nothing wrong.'

[21]"Under three things the earth trembles, under four it cannot bear up:[22]a servant who becomes king, a godless fool who gets plenty to eat, [23]a contemptible woman who gets married, and a servant who displaces her mistress.

[24]"Four things on earth are small, yet they are extremely wise: [25]Ants are creatures of little strength, yet they store up their food in the summer; [26]hyraxes are creatures of little power, yet they make their home in the crags; [27]locusts have no king, yet they advance together in ranks; [28]a lizard can be caught with the hand, yet it is found in kings' palaces.

[29]"There are three things that are stately in their stride, four that move with stately bearing: [30]a lion, mighty among beasts, who retreats before nothing; [31]a strutting rooster, a he-goat, and a king secure against revolt.

[32]"If you play the fool and exalt yourself, or if you plan evil, clap you hand over your mouth!

[33]For as churning cream produces butter, and as twisting the nose produces blood, so stirring up anger produces strife."

Month One Journal Entry   Date: _____

_____

_____

_____

_____

_____

_____

_____

_____

_____

Month Two Journal Entry   Date: _____

_____

_____

_____

_____

_____

_____

_____

_____

_____

Month Three Journal Entry   Date: _____

_____

_____

_____

_____

_____

_____

_____

_____

_____

Month Four Journal Entry   Date: _____

_____

_____

_____

_____

_____

_____

_____

_____

_____

_____

Month Five Journal Entry   Date: _____

_____

_____

_____

_____

_____

_____

_____

_____

_____

_____

_____

Month Six Journal Entry   Date: _____

_____

_____

_____

_____

_____

_____

_____

_____

_____

_____

_____

Month Seven Journal Entry   Date: _____

_____

_____

_____

_____

_____

_____

_____

_____

_____

Month Eight Journal Entry   Date: _____

_____

_____

_____

_____

_____

_____

_____

_____

_____

_____

Month Nine Journal Entry   Date: _____

_____
_____
_____
_____
_____
_____
_____
_____
_____
_____

Month Ten Journal Entry   Date: _____

_____
_____
_____
_____
_____
_____
_____
_____
_____
_____

Month Eleven Journal Entry   Date: _____

_____
_____
_____
_____
_____
_____
_____
_____
_____
_____

Month Twelve Journal Entry   Date: _____

_____
_____
_____
_____
_____
_____
_____
_____
_____
_____
_____

The Thirty-First
Destiny

"Speak up for those who cannot speak for themselves; ensure justice for those being crushed. Yes, speak up for the poor and helpless, and see that they get justice."
~Proverbs 31:8-9 (NLT)

The Book of Proverbs concludes with this chapter written by King Lemuel, inspired by the teachings of his mother. Some scholars suggest that Lemuel was his mother's affectionate name for King Solomon. Others suggest it refers to King Hezekiah, but there is no definitive proof of further identity anywhere in Scripture. In Hebrew, his name means "to God," as in belonging to God, or "for God." We must just accept that Lemuel was a wise king in his own right, since the Holy Spirit saw fit to have his writings in the book. And what mother wouldn't be blessed to have the words of life she spoke into her son treasured and memorialized by him for the benefit of millions through the years?

This chapter has classic verses pointed to for the excellent attributes of a wife. I encourage you to look deeper, though, as you read. Look beyond it as a list of "shoulds" to see what God speaks through Lemuel's writings from the very first verse. I'm confident you'll recognize that, whether man or woman, Proverbs 31 is about choosing to walk in destiny.

These writings begin with words of wisdom about the behavior of kings. He is warned to not waste his time on frivolous relationships with women, to stay away from strong drink, to speak for those who have no voice and to promote equity. As you read, note why his mother says these things. She is not asking for blind obedience to concepts she has randomly conceived, but she is speaking life into his future and his legacy. Each instruction, if not correctly applied, will divert him from his God-ordained destiny as a righteous leader.

The rest of the chapter speaks of a virtuous and capable wife. To my sisters reading this, please know that this is not a checklist of items God expects you to achieve or to force yourself to accomplish all at once during your marriage. Yes, there are certain core spiritual values and points of integrity we read about, but we are not all expected to get up before dawn to prepare breakfast for our household, manage the children, negotiate grand business deals, all while burning our lamps working late into the night. Trying to check these items off some grand list "because we have to" can be exhausting. This speaks instead of actions that flow from a mind and heart aligned with Wisdom, knowing what is good and right for *her* to do. It's like an elegant, limitless buffet that we approach with a fine porcelain plate. The plate is not designed to have food just piled on it in gluttonous, overwhelming fashion. We are not necessarily called to take one of everything. We approach the buffet in a spirit of non-competition because the buffet is always refreshed and there is always enough. We carefully select the items that are right for us, while appreciating the beauty of those items that are better enjoyed by others. It's okay for us to enjoy the items on our plate, allowing them to provide nourishment to our own hope and spirit. Therein lies the beauty when we each walk in the individual destiny given to us by God.

And so, we close the month well-rounded in awareness of wisdom, knowledge and understanding. Well done! Absorb what God has spoken to you this month, and tomorrow we'll find each other back at Proverbs 1. Be sure to read Chapter 32 after journaling today.

Proverbs Chapter 31
(NLT)

[1]The sayings of King Lemuel contain this message, which his mother taught him.

[2]O my son, O son of my womb, O son of my vows, [3]do not waste your strength on women, on those who ruin kings.

[4]It is not for kings, O Lemuel, to guzzle wine. Rulers should not crave alcohol.

[5]For if they drink, they may forget the law and not give justice to the oppressed.

[6]Alcohol is for the dying, and wine for those in bitter distress.

[7]Let them drink to forget their poverty and remember their troubles no more.

[8]Speak up for those who cannot speak for themselves; ensure justice for those being crushed.

[9]Yes, speak up for the poor and helpless, and see that they get justice.

[10]Who can find a virtuous and capable wife? She is more precious than rubies.

[11]Her husband can trust her, and she will greatly enrich his life.

[12]She brings him good, not harm, all the days of her life.

[13]She finds wool and flax and busily spins it.

[14]She is like a merchant's ship, bringing her food from afar.

[15]She gets up before dawn to prepare breakfast for her household and plan the day's work for her servant girls.

[16]She goes to inspect a field and buys it; with her earnings she plants a vineyard.

[17]She is energetic and strong, a hard worker.

[18]She makes sure her dealings are profitable; her lamp burns late into the night.

[19]Her hands are busy spinning thread, her fingers twisting fiber.

[20]She extends a helping hand to the poor and opens her arms to the needy.

²¹She has no fear of winter for her household, for everyone has warm clothes.

²²She makes her own bedspreads. She dresses in fine linen and purple gowns.

²³Her husband is well known at the city gates, where he sits with the other civic leaders.

²⁴She makes belted linen garments and sashes to sell to the merchants.

²⁵She is clothed with strength and dignity, and she laughs without fear of the future.

²⁶When she speaks, her words are wise, and she gives instructions with kindness.

²⁷She carefully watches everything in her household and suffers nothing from laziness.

²⁸Her children stand and bless her. Her husband praises her: ²⁹"There are many virtuous and capable women in the world, but you surpass them all!"

³⁰Charm is deceptive, and beauty does not last, but a woman who fears the Lord will be greatly praised.

³¹Reward her for all she has done. Let her deeds publicly declare her praise.

Month One Journal Entry   Date: _____

_____
_____
_____
_____
_____
_____
_____
_____
_____
_____

Month Two Journal Entry   Date: _____

_____
_____
_____
_____
_____
_____
_____
_____
_____
_____
_____

Month Three Journal Entry   Date: _____

_____
_____
_____
_____
_____
_____
_____
_____
_____
_____

Month Four Journal Entry   Date: _____

_____
_____
_____
_____
_____
_____
_____
_____
_____
_____

Month Five Journal Entry   Date: _____

_____

_____

_____

_____

_____

_____

_____

_____

_____

_____

Month Six Journal Entry   Date: _____

_____

_____

_____

_____

_____

_____

_____

_____

_____

_____

_____

Month Seven Journal Entry   Date: _____

_____
_____
_____
_____
_____
_____
_____
_____
_____
_____
_____

Month Eight Journal Entry   Date: _____

_____
_____
_____
_____
_____
_____
_____
_____
_____
_____

Month Nine Journal Entry   Date: _____

_____

_____

_____

_____

_____

_____

_____

_____

_____

_____

Month Ten Journal Entry   Date: _____

_____

_____

_____

_____

_____

_____

_____

_____

_____

_____

Month Eleven Journal Entry   Date: _____

_____
_____
_____
_____
_____
_____
_____
_____
_____
_____

Month Twelve Journal Entry   Date: _____

_____
_____
_____
_____
_____
_____
_____
_____
_____

Chapter 32
Living in Practice

"But solid food is for full-grown men, for those whose senses and mental faculties are <u>trained by practice</u> to discriminate and distinguish between what is morally good and noble and what is evil and contrary either to divine or human law."
~Hebrews 5:14 (AMPC)

Congratulations! You've pursued Wisdom to the month's end. Whether you began this journey on the first or at some other point in the month, whether you participated every day or less frequently, you *have* begun a <u>practice</u> in wisdom that has the potential to reverberate throughout your days and can echo into your future generations through the life you live and the legacy you leave.

It's so very important to continue your practice! Remember, committing to a practice is a form of continually training ourselves in an ongoing exercise that advances us in the knowledge and skill of a thing. The thing we are growing in knowledge and skill of here is Wisdom. Tomorrow we continue our practice as we turn back to Chapter 1: "The First" and begin journaling with a new month of entries. Every day that we read a chapter of Proverbs is another opportunity to grow in our relationship with God. Truly seek Him daily. Ask Him for wisdom, ask Him for new insight. Ask Him to expand your knowledge and understanding. Believe that He will do it as you dedicate time to study with Him. Write down the verses that speak to you each day, for the scriptures we are drawn to are never by coincidence. They are often just what we need for a certain season of life.

Developing a daily practice of filling our minds, hearts and souls with words of wisdom is an exercise that benefits more than just the invisible, spiritual woman or man that we are. A daily practice builds our discipline, our will, our ability to reason well, and a storehouse of wealth in knowledge and understanding that we constantly draw from.

We've read this month how the wise person's thoughts and actions come from a place of harmony and order, aligned with the Holy Spirit. Actions that have their root in that place of alignment with God benefit the people around us as they translate from learned knowledge to demonstrated action that positively impacts the world. Each day we can bring increase to our storehouse, allowing us to better see with wise eyes, to better speak words of life, to better act in love and righteousness. How could we *not* want to pursue wisdom's path to constantly grow and increase in these good things?

Lacking that constant training, our alignment with wisdom may shift just slightly, like the alignment on the wheels of our car. One day we are driving down the road, not even needing to touch the steering wheel to keep going perfectly straight. Then we run over a rock or take a little bounce in a hole that seems meaningless to us, but now our tires may be pulling just slightly to one side. We barely notice the change while we keep our hands on the steering wheel. The misalignment does not correct itself, though. It continues to get more severe by degrees that pull the car further and further to the one side until we must bring it to the mechanic to be corrected and properly aligned once more.

Think of the alignment of our senses and mental faculties in the same way. We all know the five basic human senses: sight, touch, taste, hearing, smell; but we have spiritual sense, too, that needs to be continually trained in the things of the Spirit. The Holy Spirit guides our intuition, which is one of our mental faculties. Our other mental faculties – memory, reason, the will (which helps us exercise discipline in our lives), perception (seeing and evaluating through eyes of truth, not tainted with fear or patterned behaviors), even the use of our mind's imagination to see and produce things to benefit the world around us – must be trained by practice to stay aligned with wisdom and all good things.

Establishing a practice is not "practicing." We are not in a grand classroom rehearsing *for* our lives. We are born to be engaged in our own lives and *live* them. Every day we must make choices. Every day we must be engaged and intentionally act. Every day we must live in the practice of those good things God calls us to. Foundational is the wisdom He tells us to so liberally ask for and expect. This continual personal development allows us to strengthen our inner person and align with the will of the Holy Spirit of God in us, day after day, month after month, year after year.

Be richly blessed as you continue the practice of wisdom into the new month. May you grow in knowledge, understanding and peace.

Chapter 33
Topical Reference

*T*his section of blank pages is designed for you to build your own reference of topics and verses that speak to you in a special way:

- Verses on certain subjects (love, joy, strife, wisdom, learning, etc.) that may speak to you in this season of life.
- Verses that motivate you to pray in a certain way.
- Topics that God is speaking to you about, that you want to be able to find easily.
- Promises of God that you want to remember.

For example, if the meaning of the word *integrity* spoke to me, I might make an entry with a promise like what is written below, listing other chapters and verses as I continue to come across the word:

Integrity = having completeness, being undivided or whole. "The godly walk with integrity; blessed are their children who follow them." ~Proverbs 20:7 (NLT). Proverbs 10:29, 11:20

_____

_____

_____

_____

_____

_____

_____

_____

_____

_____

_____

_____

_____

_____

_____